SCHEDULED CASTES OF INDIA

DIMENSIONS OF SOCIAL CHANGE

Scheduled Castes of India

DIMENSIONS OF SOCIAL CHANGE

DR. SORAN SINGH

Gian Publishing House

29/6 SHAKTI NAGAR • DELHI-110007 • INDIA

ISBN : 978-81-212-0084-4

Published, 2018

Published by

Gyan Publishing House
5, Ansari Road
Daryaganj, New Delhi-110002
Phone: 011-47034999, 9811692060
www.gyanbooks.com
E-mail: books@gyanbooks.com

Printed at: G. Print Process, Delhi.

Preface

THE PRESENT WORK is a study in the changing socio-economic condition of the scheduled castes with special reference to district Jaunpur in eastern Uttar Pradesh. The scheduled castes which comprise a number of traditionally low order castes, have been the virtual underdogs of the Hindu society. They were known as 'Shudras' and were kept out of the mainstream of Hindu social life. However, with the emergence of modern social forces as a result of India's contact with the west, a gradual change started taking place in the attitude of caste Hindus towards these castes. After independence and especially after the establishment of a democratic republic of India, a number of steps were taken both by the Central and State Government to raise their socio-economic status and towards this end, numerous facilities were extended to them. The aim of this study is to assess the changes that have taken place in the life of the scheduled castes as a result of the socio-political changes in India in recent years.

The study is divided into fourteen chapters. Chapter I is concerned with a general discussion of the position of the scheduled castes and chapter II deals with the problem of research design and methodology. Chapter III discusses the social background of the scheduled castes and chapter IV with their social organisation in its various dimension. Chapter V analyses the occupational mobility of the respondents in three generations and chapter VI deals with their economic conditions. Chapters VII is concerned with their education, political participation and political affiliation. Chapter VIII presents the new dimensions of social change among scheduled castes, And chapters IX to XII respectively deal with a study of intercaste relations and social distance among scheduled castes, the changing socio-economic conditions of the scheduled castes in Jaunpur district, indebtedness among scheduled castes, and weaker sections in India and reform movements. Chapter XIV is a brief retrospect of the main findings of the study and a summary of its main conclusions.

A number of friends-officials and non officials have helped me in the course of this study. It is not possible for me to acknowledge my debt to them all individually. But I am particularly grateful to the authorities of the Collectorate Library, Jaunpur, of the Lucknow University, Tagore Library, Gorakhpur University Library, U.P. Government Secretariate Library and T.D. College Library, Jaunpur. I am also thankful to my respondents who gave me full co-operation in the collection of first hand data concerning the various aspects of their life. My thanks are due also to Shri Hridya Narain Singh, Ex-M.L.C., Ex-Principal, Pro-vice Chanceller, T.D. College, Jaunpur and to my guide Dr. S.P. Nagendra, M.A. Ph.D., Professor and Head of the Department of Sociology, University of Gorakhpur who have helped me in ways too numerous to specify.

SORAN SINGH

Head
P.G. Dept. of Sociology
T.D. College, Jaunpur

Contents

Chapter One

The Scheduled Castes

The Hindu social organisation was traditionally divided into the two main substrata known respectively as 'Dwij' and 'Shudra'. Since the distinction between the two was based on ritual consideration, any contact or social intercourse between the two was wholly out of the question. The distance between the two substrata was considered so important that a whole group of taboos and restrictions was prescribed for maintaining and perpetuating it. The well-known commensal and connubial restrictions prevailing in the caste system had precisely this function to perform namely to perpetuate the discontinuity of the 'Dwijas' and the 'Shudras'. The 'Dwijas' comprised the three upper caste Hindus—the 'Brahmins', the 'Kshatriyas' and the 'Vaishayas', with their further subdivisions while the 'Shudras' consisted of the lower castes who were placed at the bottom of the social hierarchy. It is, needless, to discuss the basis of this rigid bifurcation of the Hindu society; it has persisted till modern times with all its consequences.

With the gradual erosion of the ritual base of the traditional Hindu society for which a number of factors are responsible, the distinction between the two, the upper and the lower castes and especially between the 'Shudras' and the caste Hindus tended to acquire a predominantly social and economic character and in this process became more rigid. This resulted in a further worsening of the position of the lower castes. The lower castes by virtue of their low gradation in the Hindu social order in due course of time were denied access to religious places, and watering points were, also, not allowed to sit inside a school house, but had to remain outside lest their contact should contaminate the upper caste Hindus. In addition to these, they also suffered other social disabilities. They had to use separate wells and were debarred from public utilities, such as the use of roads and tanks.[1] They were denied the services of the barbers and their admission to tea shops, hotels or theatres owned by private individuals were also prohibited.

These lower castes were variously known until the eighteenth century as 'broken man', 'untouchable', 'out caste', 'pamchamas', 'atisudras', 'avarnas', 'antyajas', 'namshudras', 'pariahas', 'unseeables' and 'unapproachables'. In British officialese sometime late in the last century the term 'depressed classes' was introduced and remained the most commonly used, though vague name of the group for many decades,[2] till the census report of India; 1931 proposed the new term 'exterior class' for this label. The term was used mainly to refer to those groups which had been cast away from the Hindu society for some breach of caste rules. In the 1931 census, special efforts were also made to draw up a schedule of these castes so that they could be favoured with special privileges. The same year at the Round Table Conference in London, Dr. Ambedkar also demanded a change of nomenclature for these castes. He proposed that the untouchables be called protestant Hindus or non-conformist Hindus. Ambedkar also sought at the conference a separate electorate for the untouchables and won his point. Gandhiji opposed it and went on his historic fast which was followed by the Poona pact signed on 24th September, 1932.

The following resolution was adopted at the conference :

"The conference resolves that henceforth amongst Hindus no one shall be regarded as an untouchable by reason of his birth and that those who have been so regarded hitherto will have the same right as Hindus in regard to the use of public roads and all other public institution. This right shall have statutory recognition at the opportunity and first be one of the earliest acts of the Swarajya Parliament if it shall not have received such recognition before that time.

It is further agreed that it shall be the duty of all Hindu leaders to secure by every legitimate and peaceful means, an early removal of all social disabilities now imposed by custom upon the so-called untouchable classes, including the bar in respect of admission to temples."

It is a rather significant fact that the word scheduled caste was first coined by the Simon Commission and incorporated in the Government of India Act 1935, Section 279.[3] During a celebrated temple entry campaign in 1933, Gandhi bestowed on the untouchables the new name of 'Harijan', meaning thereby the children of God which he took from a poem by a sage in his native place Gujarat. For the promotion of the uplift of Harijans, he also started a publication called the 'Harijan'.

Gandhi's followers accepted the new nomenclature and it soon passed into common usage in our country inspite of the fact that some leaders of the ex-untouchables like Jagjivan Ram did not like the term. We have shown above how the term 'scheduled castes' came to be applied to the 'Shudras'. It is a significant fact that the new nomenclature was adopted during the British rule. For India's contact with the west in the eighteenth century, which was responsible for bringing about a new social climate in India, was made possible only through the British rule. It was during the British rule that attempts were made by the English educated intelligentsia to do away with the restrictions prevailing in the caste system and to assimilate the untouchables into the fold of higher Hinduism.

The Britishers brought with them a casteless culture and liberal education which provided full scope to individual liberty. Some outstanding personalities like Raja Ram Mohan Roy, Keshab Chandra Sen and Debendra Nath Tagore in their close contact and were so much influenced by them that they started movements which aimed at liberalizing the Hindu religion and practising open fraternity. In 1828, Raja Ram Mohan Roy founded the Brahmo Samaj and through it established a brotherhood wherein members will not be divided on the caste basis. One positive aspect of this movement was the introduction of a new social legislation legalising inter-caste marriages. Although in early 1850s, the Castes Disabilities Removal Act had already dealt a major blow at the institution of caste yet it only facilitated conversion to another religion or admission into another caste. In 1858, the Bombay Government announced that the government would refuse support to such schools where the benefits of education were with-held on account of caste or race. The special Marriage Act of 1872 also made it possible for any Indian of whatever caste or creed to contract a valid marriage with a person belonging to any caste or creed, provided the parties registered the contract of marriage declaring, *inter alia*, that they did not belong to any religion. Raja Ram Mohan Roy regretted to say that the present system of religion adhered to by the Hindus was not well calculated to promote their political interest. The distinction of castes introducing innumerable divisions and sub-divisions among them had entirely deprived them of political feeling and the multitude of religious rites and ceremonies and the laws of purification had totally disqualified them from understanding any difficult enterprise. It was, therefore, necessary that some changes should take place in their religion, at least for the sake of their political advantage and social comfort.[4]

The death of the founder was almost fatal to the infant society, but the munificence of his friend prince Dwarka Nath Tagore enabled it to exist until a better day dawned.[5] Two young friends -- Debendra Nath Tagore and Keshab Chandra joined the Samaj. A new period of growth and fruitful labour followed. Debendra Nath Tagore was very much of a Hindu in feeling and believed that, however, evil caste might be, members of the Samaj ought not be compelled, in the circumstances of those to give it up. He was opposed to marriages between people of different castes and he could not endure the thought of widow re-marriage. Keshab Chandra, on the other hand, wanted to see the overthrow of the caste system and the complete reform of the Hindu Polity.

Raja Ram Mohan Roy laid the foundations of modern Indian nationalism by insisting that a free society demanded a free society and a free society postulated the free individual and the freedom of the individual meant to him, the capacity of taking well-formed judgements about the affairs of his state and the moral capacity to stand courageously by them.[6]

The disagreement between the late Raja's friends led to the formation of two parties within the Samaj.[7] Debendra Nath Tagore led the Ādi Samaj which adopted the retention of Hindu usages and customs, and the observance of social distinctions such as those obtaining in the caste system. Keshab Chandra being more under Christian influence formed the Brahmo Samaj of India (Sadharan Samaj) and invited all to join it. Until his death in

1884, he retained his primacy in Brahmaism by the sheer genuis and force of his character and castigated idolatory, polytheism, orthodoxy, untouchability and child marriage with an extra-ordinary freshness of his thinking and writing.

The Prarthana Samaj founded by Sindhis, Parsis, and Marathis also, gave a big joint to the old Hindu traditions and institutions. The notable pioneers of this movement were men like M.G. Ranade, Sir N.G. Chandavarkar, R.G. Bhandarkar and Agrakar who were all for remodelling the Hindu society. They were the sober realists who endeavoured to establish a nexus between the present and the future rather than between the past and the future. If they looked to the past, it was not to idealize it but to see how it could be accommodated to suit the needs of the present.[8] The Prarthana Samaj met in a conference at Allahabad in December, 1910 and they passed the resolution that efforts should be made to improve the moral material and social conditions of the lower castes and urged that further attempts be made to obtain for these castes full recognition as an integral part of the general body of the community. The conference also recorded its opinion that no attempts should be made in the census to introduce artificial distinctions among castes recognised as belonging to our community.[9]

In the Punjab, the Deo Samaj too, was inspired by the ideals of the Brahmo Samaj but it could not gain any momentum there. The Deo Samaj came into being on the Queen's jubilee day February 16, 1887 and Shiva Narayan Agnihotri led it. Until 1913, all went fairly well with the Samaj; it was entirely devoted to the service of the world and stood for the establishment of the kingdom of Truth and Godness on this earth. The aims and objects of the Samaj were very similar to those of the Brahmo Samaj. Until 1886, it was an organ of the Sadharan Brahmo Samaj in Calcutta.

During the year 1875, Swami Dayanand (original name Mulshankar) established the Arya Samaj with a view to reconstructing the Hindu society. He had a vision of India, purged of her superstitions filled with the fruits of science, worshipping one God, fitted for self-rule, having a place in the sisterhood of nations and restored to her ancient glory.[10] To accomplish his splendid dream, he dealt heavy blows at the accumulated superstitions of the centuries and the Brahmanical church as did Luther at the Roman church. His idea was to see India rejuvenated and revitalized socially, religiously and politically. He wanted to eliminate the differences of caste and class in order to make the people of India socially one.[11]

Instead of recognising birth as the basis of caste, he suggested 'guna' (character), 'karm' (action), 'swabhava' (nature) as the criteria of caste. He maintains that those born as Brahmans who performed good deeds are, no doubt, Brahmans but the low born, also, whose merits, temperament and vocation are like those of the higher varnas are equally high born as are the higher varnas. This means that a man or a woman should belong to the varna for which he or she is fit.[12] Dayananda also warned the caste Hindus that the upper castes should bear in mind that if their children remained ignorant, they would have to go down to the level of the shudra and the lower castes likewise would go up to the level of higher castes if their performance was good.

Swami Dayananda denounced untouchability as inhuman and derogatory to the fair name of the Vedic religion. Untouchability was not divinely ordained ; it was largely due to bad environment, association and training and the resulting deterioration of character. In this respect, Dayananda became the forerunner of Mahatma Gandhi, who too, devoted his life to the cause of the untouchables.[13]

Both sets of ideas, traditional and modern seem to have been firmly implanted in Dayananda's mind. He had a keen desire to obtain for India all the advantages which western civilization had conferred on the nations, Europe and America. For this he established his contact with the Theosophical society which had been founded in New York in 1875. In 1878 the founder of the society, Col. Olcott and Madame Blavatskey suggested a union of the two movements – the Arya Samaj and the Theosophical society. The theosophist leaders came to India in January 1879 and the strange union continued under 1881 when it was broken off, both parties feeling bitter and aggrieved.[14]

Theosophy as a system of religion, science and practical life was carried much further by Mrs. Annie Beasant and C.W. Leadbeater in India. By the year 1884, the Theosophical society had attained great success. Mrs Beasant decried the obscurantist practices of Hindu society and pleaded for a synthesis of the east and the west. The Theosophical Society like the Arya Samaj aimed at bettering the conditions of the untouchables and creating in them a consciousness for their rights. Other militant movements against the rigid order of caste were led by Jyotir Phooley of Poona, and A. B. Lathe. In 1873, Phooley established the Satya Shodhak Samaj for asserting the worth of man irrespective of his caste. He started a primary school for the benefit of the untouchables in Poona. The Maharaja of Kolhapur, later, infused a new life in this agitation. In his writings he demanded representation for all castes of the Hindus in all the local bodies, government services and other institutions. A.B. Lathe, likewise, desired the total disappearance of caste barriers. Some social workers like V.R. Shinde and A.V. Thakkar also roused the feelings of the caste Hindus against the unjust doctrine of untouchability. Their demand for the removal of untouchability assumed a national character and their many pronged attack on the caste system helped a lot in changing the view point of many high caste Hindus. The government resolution in 1923 also, assisted a great deal in combating the old ideas about the untouchables. The resolution maintained that no grants would be paid to any aided educational institution which refused admission to the depressed class students. As a result of this policy of government, the practice of segregating the depressed classes began to disappear fast. Like the Bombay government, the Madras government also enforced the right of the depressed classes (Dalit Varga) to equal treatment in 1923. The Vaikam movement of Travancore in 1924 further manifested a determined effort of the depressed classes to pass through the main roads of the city. In 1925, the Madras legislative council introduced a bill which threw open all public places to all classes of people including the depressed classes. As a result of such measures, many caste Hindus felt pride in having tea with them. In Mahad and Nagpur, the prominent depressed class-leader Dr. Ambedkar led his castemen in 1923 for asserting their rights.[15] Inspite of the many movements organised by religious and political leaders and legal measures adopted by the government, the position of the scheduled castes had probably altered very little until the dawn of independence. Thus, the Hindu wrote in 1932 on the plight of the untouchables : "In this Tinnevelly district, there is a class of unseeables, called Purada Vannans. They are not allowed to come out during day time because their sight is considered to be pollution".[16] In a publication of the same year Ghurye likewise observed that the untouchables in many areas could not have music at their own private festivals; such as, weddings. They could not enter any Hindu temples, caste Hindu houses or other establishment or take water from the common village wells.[17] In Gujarat these lower castes used to wear a horn as their distinguishing mark.[18] The Brahmans of Travancore as in most of other parts of India had taken care to take the maximum exemption from punishment, at least, their sentence was far more lenient than that passed on the other castes for the same crimes.[19] The houses of the depressed caste people were generally separated from those of other castes, in fact, they were clustered and set apart from those of other castes. Government and corporations had been known to allot separate chawls to caste Hindus and depressed classes : generally separate chawls were assigned to the depressed castes.[20] J.H. Hutton wrote in 1946, that the Kallar in Ramnad propounded eight prohibitions, the disregard of which led to the use of violence by the Kallar against the exterior castes whose huts were fired, whose granaries and property were destroyed, and whose livestock was looted. The eight prohibitions were as follows :

(1) that the Adi-Dravids shall not wear ornaments of gold and silver;[21]

(2) that the males should not be allowed to wear their clothes below their knees or above the hips;

(3) that their males should not wear coats or shirts or baniyans;

(4) that no Adi-Dravida shall be allowed to have his hair cropped;

(5) that the Adi-Dravidas should not use other than earthen vessels in their homes;

(6) that their women shall not be allowed to cover the upper portion of their bodies no clothes or ravukvais or thavanies;

(7) that their women shall not use umbrellas for protection against sun and rain, nor should they wear sandals;

The lower castes could not satisfactorily observe the above prohibitions. The Kallar again met together and framed eleven prohibitions as below :

(1) The Adi-Dravids and Devendrakula Vellars should not wear clothes below their knees.

(2) The men and women of the above castes should not wear gold jewels.

(3) The women should carry water only in mud pots and not in copper or brass vessels. They should use straw only to carry the waterpots and no clothes should be used for that purpose.

(4) Their children should not read and get themselves educated.

(5) Their men and women should work as slaves of the Mirasdars in their respective pannars.

(6) They should not cultivate the land either on waram or lease from the Mirasdars.

(7) Their children should be asked only to tend the cattle of the Mirasdars.

(8) They must sell away their own lands to Mirasdars of the village at very cheap rates, and if they do not do so, no water will be allowed to them to irrigate their lands. Even if something is grown by the help of rain water, the crops should be robbed away, when they are ripe for harvest.

(9) They must work as coolies from 7 A.M. to 6 P.M. under the Mirasdars and their wages shall be for men Re. 0.40 per day and for women Re. 0.20 per day.

(10) The above said communities should not use Indian music (Malam etc.) in their marriages and other celebrations.

(11) They must stop their habit of going on a horse in procession before tying the Holy thread in marriage, and they must use their house-doors as a palanquin for the marriage processions and no vehicle should be used by them for any purpose.

In some places the high castes took good care to see that the depressed classes people did not develop notions of self respect. They would not allow them to assume decent names; nor would they permit them to dress after the manner of the high caste Hindus. Whilst in most of the parts of the country, humiliating restrictions had vanished; in the hills and other inaccessible places conditions continued to be much the same as in the past.[22] In Kangra district, depressed class women were not allowed to wear flounces deeper than four inches to their dress, not to use gold ornaments. Restrictions similar in nature were also found in Tehri Garhwal. A depressed class man could not keep sitting when a high caste man passed by. Even in cities the orthodox Hindu did not treat educated members of the depressed classes, on the same footing as the educated members of the high castes. Usually, these people had separate kachha wells. In some areas of western U.P., the 'Chamars' and 'Dhobis' were allowed to use wells of the high caste people, provided they used metal utensils for drawing water. But this concession was not extended to the Bhangis. They were not always treated well in hospitals, partly because they belonged to the dumb millions and partly because of the prejudices of high caste Hindu underlings. In the Punjab, they were statutorily debarred from acquiring proprietary rights in agriculture but they could buy land only for non-agricultural purposes. They were probably prevented from taking to any of the more lucrative callings.[23]

Independence in 1947 brought many promises for these people in the field of politics. A number of provisions were incorporated in the new Indian Constitution for the protection of the Harijans. Article 341 of the Constitution was promulgated on the 26th of January, 1950 which affirmed that the people of India had constituted themselves into a sovereign 'Democratic-Republic'. As per Article I of the Constitution, the state would secure to all its citizens justice, liberty and equality and promote fraternity among various communities living in the republic of India.

The Government of India also appointed a committee under the chairmanship of Shri R.R. Diwakar in August 1950 to examine the possibility of abolishing caste and communal distinctions altogether. The committee in its confidential report suggested that a bill should be brought forward rendering the recording of caste and sub-caste in a deed for registration, unnecessary. The Late Pt. Jawaharlal Nehru in 1952 openly condemned the caste loyalty of the Bihar Ministry and declared as the president of the Congress that persons thinking and acting on castelines should be expelled from the party forthwith. After the Avadi session of the Congress party, the Congress high command started thinking most seriously in the direction of eliminating caste loyalty.

The appointment of a Commissioner for scheduled castes and scheduled tribes to look after the interests and welfare of these people was a landmark in the history of the country. The Commissioner has been issuing his report regarding the Harijans and Scheduled Tribes' welfare since 1951 under article 333 of the Constitution.

The Untouchability Act, 1955 or Act No. XXII of 1955 was still further, step towards the removal of the social disabilities of the scheduled castes. Now under this act, the religious disabilities, such as; non-access to the temples or holy shrines etc. and social disabilities like non-access to public places, shops and watering places are treated as cognisable offences punishable with imprisonment upto six months and fine upto Rs. 500. The act outlaws the imposition of disabilities or grounds of untouchability virtually in all fields of activity, excepting homelife, private religious ceremonies and private employment. The U.O.A. thus punishes not only the direct enforcement of disabilities but also indirect social support of untouchability.[24]

Besides, seats have also been reserved in the Central and state legislatures for these people roughly in proportion to their population. Representation of the Harijans by election nomination or cooptation has been ensured at all levels in almost every state where Panchayati Raj has been introduced. They are also accorded preferential treatment in the matter of education. A considerable proportion of the Plan Outlay has been allocated for their education.

Demographic Composition : Scheduled Caste

Both for social and political reasons, the demographic composition of the scheduled castes is quite interesting. The census Commissioner in 1921 put their total strength at 52,680,000.[25] This figure was 10 million more than the figures given by the Franchise Committee of 1919. It had reported their strength at 42 million.[26]

These figures do not vary much from the estimate given by the Nair Central Committee of 1929[27] (44.50 millions) but varies considerably from the estimate of the Hartog Committee[28] (30 millions). Now according to the Census Report of India, 1961,[29] the scheduled castes have a population of 6.45 crores and thus, constitute about 15 per cent of the total population of the country. More than half of this number is distributed in the four states of Uttar Pradesh (1.5 crores), West Bengal (0.69 crores), Bihar (0.65 crores) and Tamil Nadu (0.61 crores) respectively. All the four states comprise 1/5 of the total population of the scheduled castes in the country. The state of Uttar Pradesh has had the larger concentration of population which is 1,55,99,609 and thus constitutes 21 per cent of the total population of the state (7,37,26,909).[30]

The official list of the scheduled castes first published by the government in the early 1930s and revised in 1957 shows that there are 1,100 sub-divisions of these castes. If the government's listings are consolidated and their similarities are taken into account, their total number would be 405. But in their larger mass, these remain separate and distinct groups each with its own particular slice of tradition of pollution, its own set of ritually impure tasks to perform, its own local set of rules to observe, its own different local master caste not to contaminate.[31] At the present time, the scheduled castes total about 51 in the Uttar Pradesh. The following scheduled castes are now listed in the scheduled caste category in the state of Uttar Pradesh.[32]

Sl. No.	*Name of Scheduled Castes with population*	*General Description*
(1)	(2)	(3)
1.	Badhik (9,972)	They were formerly hunters and bird catchers ; now mostly cultivators and also workers in Railways.
2.	Badi (1,724)	Vagrants, professional dancers, singers, acrobats, jugglers and makers of small articles and rope-walkers.
3.	Baheliya (27,629)	Hunters and fowlers.
4.	Baiswar (5,774)	Land-holders and cultivators.

(1)	(2)	(3)
5.	Bajaniya	Vagrant dancers, acrobats, jugglers, conjurers and makers of small articles.
6.	Bajgi (2,165)	Vagrant dancers, acrobats, jugglers, conjurers and makers of small articles.
7.	Balahar (8,720)	Belong to the category of Doms, of plains-village, menials and watchmen.
8.	Balhi (902)	Cotton weavers.
9.	Balmiki (58,389)	A section of Mehtars, derives name from Valmiki saint.
10.	Banmanus (8,840)	Former name of Rajis. In eastern U.P. they are agricultural labourers and collect forest leaves for making pattals.
11.	Basod (58,805)	Belong to category of plain Doms.
12.	Beldar (59,247)	Earthworkers and stone dressers.
13.	Bhuiya (3,188)	Mostly hereditary ploughmen and agriculturists and labourers.
14.	Bhuiyar (26,766)	Weavers of coarse cloth and blankets. In Moradabad they are identified as Chamars. Instances of inter-marriage with Koris may be cited.
15.	Boria (1,173)	Village servants and cultivators.
16.	Chamars (8,693,327)	Leather workers and shoe-makers and day labourers on the fields.
17.	Chero (12,779)	An aboriginal tribe of Mirzapur, but now under the process of absorption in Hinduism.
18.	Dabgar (3,754)	Found in the Eastern U.P., make large raw hide vessels, beaten raw camel's hide vessels and bottles for ghee and oil and drum heads etc. Originally cobblers, manufacturers of leather containers for ghee and oil.
19.	Dhanger (8,705)	Ploughmen, day labourers and agricultural labourers.
20.	Dharkers (41,662)	A sub-caste of Dom, rope-makers.

(1)	(2)	(3)
21.	Dhobie (888,466)	Washermen.
22.	Dhusia	(Under Chamars) A sub-caste of Chamars, shoe-makers, harness makers and mostly day labourers.
23.	Dom (41,338)	Low professional caste of drummers, weavers, village watchman (In Eastern U.P. they are scavengers).
24.	Domar/Doris (11,081)	Acrobats, jugglers, rope-dancers, make comb broom, dolls and matress.
25.	Dusadh (93,021)	A menial caste of village watchmen and messengers.
26.	Ghorami (03)	An off-shoot of Chamar caste engaged in making raw hide jars and thatching, but in Dehradun, they are thatchers.
27.	Ghasi (1,742)	Name appears to have been derived from ghas meaning grass. They are engaged in cutting grass, tending horses and act as musicians at festivals.
28.	Gond (38,356)	A fishing and cultivating caste.
29.	Gual (314)	Vagrants, dancers, acrobats, jugglers, conjurers and makers of small articles.
30.	Hadi (2,907)	Engaged in collection and disposal of bones belong to professional caste of sweepers and scavengers called Hadi or Hari.
31.	Hela (21,051)	Scavengers.
32.	Jatawa	They are Chamars and have left skinning animals, but are leather workers.
33.	Jhusia	Shoe-makers and harness makers (synonym of Dhusia).
34.	Kanjars (31,335)	Basket, mat and rope-makers.
35.	Khatik (30,53,26)	Traditionally fruit and vegetable sellers; also butchers.

(1)	(2)	(3)
36.	Kharot (275)	Minor agriculturists.
37.	Kori	Traditionally cotton-weavers.
38.	Lalbegi (11,316)	A caste of sweepers and scavengers. They are Mohammedans, though some of them claim their descent from Muslim saint Lalbegi and follow many Hindu customs.
39.	Majhabi (255)	Chuhra among Sikh are called Mazhabis sweepers.
40.	Mushahar	A criminal tribe (now absorbed in Hinduism, rat caterer, palanquin bearers, field labourers, cultivators, cultivating and caste.
41.	Nat (51,155)	A vagrant tribe engaged in begging and acrobatic-feats.
42.	Pankana (7,703)	Work as weavers and watchmen (Mirzapur).
43.	Parahiya (583)	Originally a tribe; do little cultivation, cut and sell wood and bamboo and exchange forest produce.
44.	Pasi (22,21,136)	Hunters and agriculturists; dressers of the flour chakkis.
45.	Rawat (17,577)	A synonym for Rajis or Ashok.
46.	Sahariya (11,788)	Agricultural labourers.
47.	Samauriya (40)	A criminal tribe. It is not a caste but a confraternity.
48.	Sansi (4896)	A wandering and criminal tribe. Hunters and catchers of animals.
49.	Shilpkar (46,5,879)	Menials and artisans; class of the hills.
50.	Tarmali	Akin to Pasis.
51.	Turaiha (2071)	An offshoot of Kahars; take fruit, gardens, fisheries on contract and sell fruits.

The well-marked contours between the different scheduled castes demonstrate tacitly that they can be distinguished from one another by rights and disabilities and segregated from one another by the absence of freedom of inter-marriage. The dwindling distinctions in this century augur well for tomorrow's India. To quote G.M. Travelyan 'national self-consciousness is beginning to dissolve the local-loyalties and the rigid class-divisions which had characterised the cosmopolitan society of the feudal age'.[33] The Ram Krishna Mission, the Arya Samaj, the Brahmo Samaj, the Servant of Indian Society, the Harijan Sewak Sangh, the Scheduled Castes Federation, the Bhartiya Depressed Classes League are some of the voluntary welfare agencies which have been carrying on the work of abolishing untouchability and they have also succeeded to a great extent in reducing the caste barriers prevailing over our society. The best way to take the wind out of the sails of the orthodox, caste people is to gain a mastery of the classical learning.[34] This seems quite impractical to-day because only those subjects can better aid and serve the needs of the scheduled castes which have professional value.

NOTES AND REFERENCES

1. (*i*) Ghurye, G.S. : Caste & Race 1932, Popular Book Depot Bombay, (The Scheduled Castes).

   (*ii*) Ambedkar, B. R., 'Who were the Shudras' (1946). Thacker and Co., Bombay.
2. Mohindra Singh : The Depressed Classes (1947), Hind Kitab Ltd., Bombay.
3. 279—(*i*) No subject of His Majesty domiciled in India shall on grounds only of religion, place of birth, descent, colour or any of them be ineligible for officer under the Crown in British India, or be prohibited on any such ground from carrying on any trade business, profession in British India.

   The Government of India Act, 1935 Section 279, Chapter V, Pt. XII. Govt. of India Press, New Delhi 1937.
4. Raja Ram Mohan Roy : English Works (1828), pp. 229-30 (Allahabad, Panani Office).
5. Farquhar, J.N. : Modern Religious Movements in India (1915), p. 39. The Macmillan Co., New York.
6. *Ibid.*, p. 43.
7. Dr. Purohit, B.R. : Hindu Revivalism and Indian Nationalism, 1965, p. 29. Sathi Prakashan, Sagar (M.P.).
8. *Ibid.*, p. 5.

9. Resolutions IV & V of the National Social Conference of the Prarthana Samaj held at Allahabad, December 1910 (ISR XXI), 221.
10. Farquhar, J.N. : Modern Religious Movements in India, p. 112.
11. Dr. Purohit, B.R. : Hindu Revivalism & Indian Nationalism, p. 34.
12. Dayananda, Swami : Satyartha Prakash, pp. 128-129. Translation by Durga Prasad. Vijanand Press, Lahore (1908).
13. Dayananda Commemoration Volume, A Tribute. The Vedic Tantralaya, Ajmer, 1933.
14. Chhajju Singh : The Life and Teachings of Swami Dayananda Saraswati, Addison Press (1903), pp. 176-532.
15. (*i*) Nargolkar, V.S. : Removal of Untouchability : Goals and Attainments. The Indian Journal of Social Work, October 1963 Vol. No. XXX Number 3.
    (*ii*) Singh, S. : New Dimensions of Untouchability—A brief Survey, Social Welfare (Hindi), Feb. 1970.
16. The Hindu, December 24, 1932.
17. Ghurye, G.S. : Caste & Race, 1932 Popular Book Depot Bombay.
18. Forbes, James : Oriental Memories, 1934, p. 238.
19. *Ibid.*, p. 256.
20. See. V.N. Varve's article : 'How far it is true, in the Social Welfare (Bombay) of 12th June, 1941 and quoted in the Depressed Classes' by Mohindra Singh, pp. 182-183.
21. Hutton, J.H. : Caste in India, Cambridge, 1946, p. 206.
22. Mohindra Singh : The Depressed Classes, 1947 Hind Kitab Ltd., Bombay, p. 143.
23. *Ibid.*, pp. 142-43.
24. (*i*) The Untouchability Act, 1955.
    (*ii*) The Protection of Civil Rights Act, 1976 has further strengthened the rights of the Harijans for social utilities.
25. Census of India, 1921, Vol. I, Part I, Para 193.
26. Franchise Committee of 1919.
27. Nair Central Committee, 1929.
28. Hartog Committee.
29. Census Report of India, 1961.
30. *Ibid.*
31. (*i*) Harold R. Issacs : India's Ex-Untouchables (1965), p. 29. Asia Publishing House, Bombay.
    (*ii*) P. L. Sen Devi : "Welfare of the Scheduled Castes and Scheduled Tribes in Kerala" Social Welfare, Jan. 1971, Vol. XVII No. 10, pp. 10, 11, 19. (Every seventh person in India on an average belongs to the

scheduled castes category. 90 per cent of the scheduled castes resides in rural areas).

32. (*i*) A Preliminary Appraisal of the Scheduled Castes of India (Office of the Registrar-General India, New Delhi).
 (*ii*) Government of India, Ministry of Law (Legislative Department).
 (*iii*) Government of India, Ministry of Home Affairs Notification No. SRO 2477A, the 29th October, 1956.
33. Trevelyan, G.M., English Social History (1944).
34. B. V. S. Patrudu : "Scheduled Castes in India : Social Progress and Social Legislation, Social Welfare : January, 1971.

Note : Uttam and Anuradha Bhirta in the Dalit Sahitya Movement (DLM) in Maharashtra : A Sociological Analysis, in Sociological Bulletin Vol. 26 No. 1 March, 1977 Observe that DLM has been reaffirming the solidarity of Harijans and rejuvenating their ideological Commitments and helping in formulating their further policies and strategies.

CHAPTER TWO

Research Design and Methodology

IN THIS ENQUIRY an attempt has been made to analyse the changes in the socio-economic conditions of the scheduled castes with particular reference to Jaunpur district in eastern U.P. Eastern Uttar Pradesh is noted for its poverty, growing pressure of population, low level of literacy and un-employment. Incidentally Jaunpur was one of the districts surveyed by the Patel Commission appointed by the Government of India to enquire into the backwardness of eastern Uttar Pradesh. In part II of this chapter we describe the ecological setting and the demographic situation of the district. According to the census report, 1961, the total population of the scheduled castes in Jaunpur district was 3,65,448. Thus, when compared to other districts, Jaunpur stands 18th in U.P. in respect of its scheduled caste population by a census study. At the same time sampling seemed an equally difficult method to use because no list of the scheduled caste families from which the units could be selected, was available. The total number of individual scheduled castes was, no doubt, available in the census report. But no information about the actual distribution in the rural or urban population could be had from any source. We, therefore, approached the District Harijan Welfare Officer in order to have some clue to the distribution of the scheduled castes in the district. The Harijan Welfare Officer also could not help us much, but he could give us the names of thirteen villages in which scheduled castes were living and which he had selected for his welfare work. This facilitated our task to some extent. We made a pilot survey of these villages and fortunately for us the survey revealed that all the scheduled castes in the district mentioned in the census report were represented in the population of the villages. We discovered that Chamars were dwelling in a cluster of 140 families in the villages, namely, Kuddupur, Ram Nagar and Khetasarai. No other scheduled castes were living in these villages. Likewise, Pasis were living in Mahimapur and Ram Nagar and their actual strength in the population of two villages was 30. No other castes were found in the village. Dhobies were found in the village Wazidpur, their actual number being 30. Musahars were living in Dhanipur and their total population was 40. In Jalalpur, Mahimapur and Lalpur, we found 30 families of Khatiks. Baheliyas were found in Sujanganj and Chak Gulam Sarwar. Their strength in the population of the two villages was 10, of which one family lived in Sujanganj and the remaining 9 lived in Chak Gulam Sarwar. Bansphors were found in Dhanipur (40). Nats lived in Taraun and their number was 20 and the Kanjars, their number was 40, were living in Kheradinganj. The Doms were, however, found on the suburb of the city and in all, there were only 20 families.

The total number of the scheduled castes found in the 13 villages, thus, came to 400. We decided to go for a census study of them all. Since the number was manageable and, also, because it looked sizeable enough to be of statistical significance we did not consider it necessary to sample it out.

All the above mentioned villages are connected with Jaunpur city either by metalled or unmetalled roads. Kuddupur looks a fairly developed village. It is electrified and connected with Jaunpur city by a metalled road. It has pucca houses and several byways inside it. The level of literacy of its inhabitants appears high. Khetasarai and Jalalpur are also electrified and are situated by the side of railway lines. Taraun, a village in Kirakat subdivision where the Nats were found has no approach roads at all. Likewise, Sujanganj is, also, located quite off the roads. Although Dhanipur is a suburb of Jaunpur city, it is neither electrified nor physically neat. It is strange that even though it is in the vicinity of the hydel electric station, it has no lights. Kheradinganj—a colony of Kanjars—is near the Marihau railway junction.

Design

The study has an exploratory design in that it does not proceed with any formal working hypothesis. It is needless to say that there are no studies of social change among scheduled castes which could serve as our guidelines in this connection. The references, that we have cited in the previous chapter and which we will have occasion to refer to, again, do give us some information about the changing position of the scheduled castes. But the findings of none of them are sociologically definitive enough to justify their acceptance as working hypotheses for a further study. Our study is therefore basically oriented to achieving some tangible results which would help in the formulation of hypothesis for further research to be undertaken in the field later.

Even so, as we have said we were not investigating a wholly untouched area. We had no doubt about the fact that changes were taking place in the socio-economic conditions of the scheduled castes, and that their social position was gradulaly improving. As we have already mentioned, the Hindu society, as a result of the interplay of a number of forces had, in the course of time itself become aware of the divisive and centrifugal tendencies existing within it and had, also, begun to realise the need to check or curb them. The various socio-religious movements which were launched in India from time to time were all oriented to the abolition of the artificial distinction between castes and specially to the amelioration of the conditions of the underdogs. In the post independent era, the state itself has taken a number of steps to raise the socio-economic status of the scheduled castes. If we go by the preamble of the constitution alone, the traditional discrimination on the basis of caste, sex and creed stands abolished now and all irrespective of their caste, religion and sex are equal before law and the state. Numerous facilities have been provided to the scheduled castes with a view to enabling them to take their rightful place in society. Legislative and executive measures have been enforced in various states to safeguard the interests of the scheduled castes in respect of land tenure, fundamental rights, social justice and education. In the all India as well state services to which recruitment is made by the Public Service Commission, reservation quotas have been fixed for the scheduled castes. The quota, which was formerly 12.5 per cent has now been raised to 15 per cent besides the 16 per cent quota fixed for services to which recruitment is made by other government agencies. Reservation quota has also been fixed in respect of seats in parliament. Other kinds of assistance for scheduled castes include grant of stipends, scholarships, freeship, mid-day-meals, uniform, exemption from payment of examination fees, book grants and hostel facilities for carrying out studies. The government has, also, made provisions in the form of grants-in-aid for the construction of houses and wells for these castes. Huge funds have been sanctioned for house construction both in rural and urban areas for them. Orders have been issued which prohibit government servants from taking begar. Instructions have also been issued to district authorities to prevent ex-zamindars from extorting begar by initiating action under section 347 of the Indian Penal Code wherever expedient. This is a measure which affects mostly the scheduled castes because all begar was generally taken from them.

Vocational schools are also being run by the government for imparting instruction in trades to the Harijans. We will try to see whether the conclusions of our study can establish that these intended changes are actually taking place or not.

Our study is mainly based on primary data which have been collected through the help of an interview schedule, combined with participant observation. The use of a questionnaire was wholly out of the question in an investigation like this whose universe consisted of illiterate people who were the headmen of their families. The interview schedule consisted of questions covering all the aspects of the subject to be investigated. An attempt was made to include as far as possible, only structured questions so that the respondents could answer them without much difficulty. Leading questions were completely avoided. The schedule was pretested before it was actually administered. During the course of filling the schedules, it was observed that some of the respondents were indifferent towards their response to the questions. They could hardly appreciate the genuine purpose of the enquiry due to their shy nature and dire illiteracy. During the interview, the investigator was mistaken for a CID man at the first instance and, therefore, in the beginning, the respondents did not co-operate with him properly. But we managed to establish close rapport with the respondents and eventually succeeded in knowing their views and attitudes in depth. We placed full reliance on the answers of the respondents although, sometimes, the authenticity of their replies was questionable.

Participant observation brought several advantages to us. One that it helped us in finding out the real feelings of the respondents in the various matters on which they were questioned and two, it gave us several additional clues to the understanding of their state of mind which could not be ascertained through interview schedule.

During the period of data collection, the informants were under the impression that the filling up of the interview schedule was important from the point of view of their social welfare. Hence they started asking question after question. How much money were they going to receive after filling the schedule. Would the government provide them with employment ? Would the government make sufficient arrangement for water supply for them ? We had no alternative but to listen to such queries patiently.

There were other respondents also who thought that the investigator had, come to obtain information about their evil practices and, therefore, they did not welcome the idea of answering the questions at all. However, on getting satisfactory assurance from the investigator, they disclosed their hearts.

As the Nats and Kanjars were always out on their errand, it was very difficult to contact them during the day time. We had, therefore, to interview them during the twilight or night.

There are areas in respect of which the information furnished by respondents could be absolutely considered correct and areas in respect of which it might be taken as only approximate. For instance the information about income and age : the respondents had a tendency to understate their income under the impression that by doing so they were making a case for more benefits coming to them from government agencies. However, efforts were made to check and cross-check the information to the extent possible. We also established contact with the 'Mukhia' or 'Sarpanch' or 'Gram Pradhan' of the village for checking certain pieces of information supplied to us by the respondents, and they fully co-operated in our venture. Besides primary data, we have made sufficient use of secondary data, also, in our study. We have used census reports, district gazetteers and the relevant publications of the government.

Tabulation and Interpretation

The information furnished by the respondents was transferred from the interview schedule to data sheets and was, then, sorted out according to age, sex, religion, caste, rural and urban differences, income etc. of the respondents. The data, thus sorted out arranged in tables for interpretation. After chapterisation was decided upon for writing the report, synoptical notes were prepared for each chapter with a view to evolving the final shade of the thesis. The conclusions arrived at, are described in the succeeding chapters.

The Field of Study : Jaunpur District

There are two divergent views with regard to the growth of Jaunpur District. It is believed that in Dvapar Yug, Maharshi Yamdagni had established his hermitage in Jamehita in a small village hardly four miles away from the city of Jaunpur. The greatest warrior of his time, Parashu Ram was also supposed to be born in this village. After the demise of the great hermit Yamdagni, the place was named Yamdagnipuri and it is this Yamdagnipuri which later grew into Jaunpur. According to the second version, during the years 1359-60, Firoz Shah Tuglaq, the Akbar of the Sultanate period established this district in his cousin's Firoz Zunar Khan's memory and named it as Zunapur after him. Jaunpur is later name for Zunapur. The district blossomed into glory and rose to the highest pinnacle of distinction during Firoz Shah Tuglaq's regime. As W. Hague observes, the region of Firoz Shah Tuglaq closes the most brilliant epoch of Muslim rule in India before the reign of Akbar.[1]

During the medieval period, the Jaunpur city enjoyed the privilege of being the capital of the Sharqi-dynasty and throughout this period, it earned the reputation of being a great seat of learning, known as, Shiraze-Hind or Darulalum. The great Sher Shah Suri had his schooling here. Sher Shah is one of those great men of history who blossomed out of dust into glory and rose to the zenith of distinction by dint of their courage, ability, resourcefulness as also by the strength of their sword. He was one of the great rulers of Delhi, and was a prince of destiny. It is also a known fact that pupils from all over the world and particularly Central Asia used to come here (Jaunpur) for the pursuit of knowledge. The great 'Shahi-Bridge' and the 'Fort' with their pristine glory owe their origin to the great king Akbar. Akbar consolidated the Mughal empire in India. Nehru wrote about him "In him the old dream of a United India took shape united not only politically in one state but originally fused into one unit."[2]

The Ecology of the District

The district of Jaunpur is bounded on the west by the district of Pratapgarh and Allahabad; on the south by Varanasi, on the east by Ghazipur, and Azamgarh and on the north by Sultanpur. It has a total area of 1555 square miles and its population is more than 18 lakhs. It has five sub-divisions, 20 parganas and 15 thanas. There has been a decrease of 9.6 square mile area since 1951 partly, on account of transfer of certain villages to other district and partly due to revised calculation of area by the board of revenue.

The district may be described as a level plain with slight undulations caused by the valleys of the rivers. All the rivers of the district flow from north-west to south-east and the slope of the country follows the same direction. The 'Gomati', the 'Sai' and the 'Bishuhi' divide the district into four almost parallel strips of the country each with fairly distinct physical characteristics. The rainfall is normally ample, the average for the last quinquennium was about 46.46.

Climate Soil and Water Resources

The climate of the district is relatively favourable. The weather is very taxing particularly in the hot summer months, from April to June. Warm winds blow, starting early in April as precursors of the monsoon. The district is exposed to river floods. The battering of the rain threatens the mud walls of the village-huts, cripples transportation and spreads sickness throughout the villages. The winter is slightly cooler and healthier. The soil is quite good and well suited for cultivation of maize, wheat and rice. The clay loam, and loam types of soil are very productive and suited for wheat-cultivation. Canals, tube-wells and lifting water schemes are the main sources of irrigation.

Communication

The villages of the district cannot be considered isolated in that, the district has several main roads leading to Varanasi, Allahabad, Lucknow and Gorakhpur. They are also connected with one another through the operation of the multi-village panchayat system. The district is also connected by railway lines with the main parts of the state.

Flora and Fauna

No important or revenue yielding forest exists in the district. The principal fruit trees are jackfruit and mango trees.

There are very few wild animals in the rural areas; monkeys are small in number and wild ducks are found only in the lake areas. Hunting these birds was formerly a favourite hobby of some people of the district. But as the lakes are being extensively used for fishery, game birds are not seen too frequently.

Administrative Institutions

The district has most of the administrative institutions, such as courts, police stations and other welfare establishments run by the government.

Ethnic Composition

Permanent residents of the district are Hindus and Muslims both. Most of these settlers are persons belonging to the Brahman, Rajput, Ahir, Kurmi, Maurya and the scheduled castes. According to 1961 census report, the population of scheduled castes in the state of Uttar Pradesh was 1,55,66,809. Jaunpur's share of this population was 3,65,448. District-wise enumeration of this is as in the table :

As the Table 1 shows, the district of Jaunpur stands 18th in the State, in respect of the population of the scheduled castes.

The castewise break-up of the scheduled castes in the district is as in the Table 2.

Religious Institutions

There are Hindus, Muslims, Sikhs, Jains and Christians in the district who assemble at their religious places for prayer. The temples are maintained by the Hindus. Temples of Hanuman Ji and Santoshi Mata are worth-mentioning where people gather on certain fixed days and offer prayers.

Mohammedans attend 'Jumma Namaj' on every Friday in the Atala-mosque. The Christians offer their prayers in their churches and the Sikhs in their Guruduaras.

TABLE 1

Showing the demographic of Jaunpur in U.P.

Sl. No.	*Name of District*	*Population of scheduled caste*
1.	Azamgarh	5,89,081
2.	Allahabad	5,86,243
3.	Basti	5,27,394
4.	Gorakhpur	5,12,262
5.	Sitapur	4,94,878
6.	Hardoi	4,87,006
7.	Meerut	4,80,128
8.	Kanpur	4,79,326
9.	Mirzapur	4,26,396
10.	Agra	4,16,539
11.	Varanasi	4,10,433
12.	Faizabad	3,98,115
13.	Bara Banki	3,94,515
14.	Rai Bareilly	3,87,110
15.	Gonda	3,80,576
16.	Saharanpur	3,79,660
17.	Aligarh	3,68,218
18.	Jaunpur	3,65,448
19.	Deoria	3,56,043
20.	Bulandshahar	3,53,420

Household Types

Most of the households are rectangular in shape and are arranged round in a square courtyard. The houses are generally built with bamboo and sangrass or tiles. The households are mostly covered by household trees. Some houses have got wooden doors and windows, but are seldom painted. The living houses of well-to-do castes are spacious and have sufficient rooms. The ordinary class of people have had two living rooms with a separate kitchen.

TABLE 2

Showing demographic composition of scheduled caste in Jaunpur District

Sl. No.	*Caste*	*Number*
1.	Bahelia	205
2.	Bharkar (Bansfod)	3,178
3.	Dhobi	15,560
4.	Dom	122
5.	Kanjar	43
6.	Khatik	8,732
7.	Musher (Banwasi)	14,431
8.	Nat	1,984
9.	Pasi	43,117
10.	Chamar (Jaiswars)	2,69,394
11.	Unclassified scheduled caste	172

Dress and Ornaments

The general mode of living is poor and the dresses of the people do not vary in any important respect from the dresses worn in other parts of the country. The dress of an average cultivator consists of a simple and coarse Dhoti fastened round the loins and falling into the knee. The quality of cloth differs according to means. Gamcha (Napkin) is commonly used here which is thrown sometimes round the body, sometimes, over the shoulders and often on the head. The majority of the people go without shoes. School-boys wear half shirt and shorts. The dress of the females consists of sari, blouse and petticoat. Footwears that are commonly used, are tyre sandals, leather sandals and rubber shoes.

Males do not wear any ornaments. Rings on the fingers are very common and so, also, earrings. A ring or an imitation jewel attached to the nose is frequently seen in the rural area. Ornaments vary with the economic conditions of the wearer and consists of gold, silver, copper, bronze and iron etc. Married Hindu females put red mark or vermillion on the forehead to show that they are married. Muslim ladies blacken their eyelids with a line of 'surma' which is a black powder made of lead and is used after mixing with oil. Both men and women use oil for anointing the head. Those who can afford, use scented oil. Soaps are used but not regularly.

Food and Drink

The cultivator of the district has nothing, except the barest necessaries which include a few earthen or metal cooking utensils, known as batli (Kettle) pan tumber and tawa for baking the bread. The food taken by the people may be considered, of ordinary type consisting principally of rice, bread, pulses, vegetables, fish and egg. In the rural area, fish and fowl are obtained ordinarily without spending any money. 'Daana' (parched maize) is very much relished by the villagers.

Beliefs and Practices

The birth of a child is always followed by great rejoicing in all communities. In case of a Hindu family, if a son is born, a ceremony known as 'Barahi' is performed on the 12th day, after the birth of the child. All marriages are settled by the father within the same community. Widow re-marriage is in practice only among the backward and scheduled castes. Dowry is common and is paid by the girl's father to the groom's father. Among the Muslims, the marriage ceremony is conducted by the 'Kazi' who reads out the 'Kalma'. All the Hindus living in the district burn the dead body while the Muslims bury the dead bodies.

The Festival-cycle

People of the district celebrate Janma Ashtami, Teej, Holi, and Deepawali with great zeal. Shrāddha, a yearly ritual occasion is also strictly observed for honouring the family dead through gifts of food to Brahmans. The 'Karva Chauth' is also celebrated by married women of all the castes. Rangoli (Hoi) is also a festival of women. They keep fast, bathe and fill two small pitchers with water. Deepawali, a festival of lights, popular all over India is one of the four main festivals of the Hindus. Makar Saṁkranti is observed by all. On Saṁkranti the Sun ceases to travel towards the inauspicious south where is the abode of death and begins to move towards the north and this changes everything. It is the great day of the year for alms giving. Basant Panchami, which means 'Yellow Fifth day' or 'Spring Fifth Day' indicates the advent of spring. People observe it by wearing yellow clothing.

Festivals celebrated in the district by the various communities do not have any untoward effect on economic production. The festival days are not workless at all. Most of the celebrations take place in the evenings. In about 1030 A.D. the Muslim Scholar Alberuni wrote an account of Indian festivals and feasts remarking that they represented cultural stability and change.[3] They are also a perennial source of amusements. On these occasions, people cut pranks and enjoy feasts and become forgetful of drudgery of daily routine of life.

NOTES AND REFERENCES

1. Hague. W. : (The Sultanate Period) Cambridge History of India, Vol. III, Cambridge 1931.
2. Nehru, Jawaharlal : Discovery of India. The Signet Press, Calcutta 1948.
3. Sachau, Edward C. (Ed.) 1910 : "Alberuni's India", London, English Translation.

CHAPTER THREE

Social Background of the Scheduled Castes

Description of Scheduled Castes

BRIEF SKETCHES of individual scheduled castes under study are given below :

The Chamars

The largest group of scheduled castes appearing under a single name 'Chamar' is a widely distributed group in U.P. It exists in various names such as, Ramdasia, Satnami and Raidan, Rohit, Rohidas, Rabidas, Ramnami and Rishi.[1] There are references to this caste even in Manu who speaks of two groups of Chamars : Karavara and Dhigvana, both being mixed in origin and concerned with leather working. The former is known as Charamkara, cutter of hides and latter who, also, is a worker and trader in leather products and is represented to-day as 'Mochi' or 'Muchi'. Baines also mentions about Rajbanshi, Koch, Bagdis, Bauris, Kaivartas. They all claim to be of Kshatriya status.[2] In earliest Rigvedic time, the leather worker does not seem to have been an object of opprobrium and, indeed, his services were of utmost importance to the warriors of his days. In the ancient Indian epic, the Mahabharata, the 'Chamar' was the maker of the shields, breast plates, and body armour as well as of drums and various parts of chariots.[3] Stink smelling of leather tanning relegated to them to the peripheries of the respectable society. They are a heterogenous group of people who have received from time to time recruits from castes higher up in the caste hierarchy.[4]

The Chamars constitute the numerically most preponderate group among the scheduled castes in the disrict with a population of 2,69,394 or 75.01 per cent of the total population of the latter. Their biggest concentration is in Khutan and Kerakat sub-divisions. The Chamars of Jaunpur district, style themselves as Jaiswars and consider themselves to be the descendants of Raja Jai Singh. Some educated youths, gave me their origin as emanating from Ravana, the great king of Lanka (now Sri Lanka) during the Ramayana period. Most of them cultivate the fields of high caste Hindus. Some of them are engaged in leather work and shoe-making.

The position of Chamar in India is very low indeed. In the villages, they work as general menials for some traditional payment in grain, clothes and food.[5] In the course of field work, however, we found the Chamars, no longer, accept payment in kind, but that insist on payment in cash for their labour. In fact, they are now in a position to bargain for their daily as well monthly wages.

There are numerous castes of Chamars. The census of 1891 listed them as many as 11,568 castes.[6]

The Pasis

They have the largest concentration in the states of Uttar Pradesh and Bihar. The word 'Pasi' is derived from the word 'pasa' meaning a noose; a loop, the rope belt. Their traditional occupation is believed to be today tapping. Thiyan and Thanan also carry on the same occupation in the south. An inscription of 11th century A.D. mentions the Idiya and Illuvas as the today tapping castes. The word 'Shanar' is from 'San' and 'nar' meaning span, long noose, this being the name in line with that of the pasi.[7] In 1874 the shanars appear to have first attempted militant assertion of their dislike of the status assigned to them by attempting to enter the Minakshi temple at Madura.[8]

The Pasis cover 11.9 per cent of the total population of the scheduled castes in the district. They claim their origin from Andheriya Kshatriya clan. They are mostly agriculturists and at some places are also known as the dressers of flour chakkies; the flour chakkies are used in rural areas for grinding the corn into flour. Before the Criminal Act was repealed, they were included in the list of criminals. The Act came into force on 31st of August, 1952.

The Dhobies

The Dhobies constitute 4.4 per cent of the total population of the scheduled castes in the district. They are engaged in their traditional occupation although some families after having shifted to urban centres have taken to laundering. They stand low in the social scale on account of their occupation. Hutton remarks, "One might have expected the washerman's to be a cleanly pursuit but the fact that it brings him contact with menstrually polluted clothes is enough to make him an outcaste, no less than the scavenger who removes night-soil or dead bodies. And in all cases, the nature of taboo is such, of course, that the contagion of the polluted occupation contaminates all members of the caste whatever their individual occupation may be and to an infinite number of generation. He further adds that this taboo is, of course, world-wide. There can be little doubt; but the reason why the objectives 'bloody' and 'bleeding' etc. are, till recently were regarded as indecent in English is because they have been used as swear (smear) words with the particular association implied.[9]

The Musahars

They comprise 4.6 per cent of the total population of the scheduled castes in the district. They were formerly considered as a tribe but were absorbed in Hinduism after the Criminal Act of 1952. They are rat-catchers, palanquin bearers, field labourers, cultivators and servile caste. Baines classes them with field labourers. The Musahars designate themselves as 'Banvasi' and hold that they are the descendants of the Banvasi[10] Raja. They fell through in their mission on account of an unavoidable adversity and thus left the woods and started eking out their subsistence by making 'dona' and 'pattals'. Dona and pattals are made of Palash leaves for serving food in them. In the Uttar Pradesh and Bihar States, they are also called 'Bengali Bagdi'. The Tamil pallan also resembles the Musahars. The word 'pallan' means the 'eater of the rat'.

The Khatiks

Demographically they are fourth in the district and constitute 2.8 per cent of the total population. At present they call themselves 'Sonkars'. They deal in pigs, grow vegetables and sell fruits.[11]

The Khatiks a sub-caste of butcher has sub-castes of Benkanwala (pork butcher), Rajgar (mason), Sombatta (rope-maker),

Mewa farosh (fruiterer), etc. Formerly fissions of this kind were often the result of migration or of political or social environmental factors, but latterly they have more often, perhaps, been the result of 'attempts' by the well-to-do elements in a despised caste to out adrift from their humbler caste brethern and raise themselves in the social scale by finding a new name, a dubious origin associating them with some higher caste.[12]

The Khatik caste has a hereditary headman called 'Chaudhari' with five panchas in Aligarh area while 'Sonkar' sub caste has a headman and six or seven panchas who are all hereditary. The Poldar sub-caste has a headman and vice-president (pradhan) both hereditary, but the Saqwa sub-caste has a headman who is elected for a single year at the Dashahra festival. In Bulandshahar, every village where the Khatiks reside, has a 'Muqaddam' who disposes of minor cases.

The Doms

The doms have been carrying on as village sweepers and scavengers. Besides, their occupation has also been singing, dancing and playing on instruments in the Punjab. But in the sub-Himalayan districts of Kumaon and Garhwal, Doms live by agriculture and village handicrafts. In Bengal, they are an immigrant caste and are assigned the work of sweeping and scavenging. In Bihar and Uttar Pradesh, they are divided into two sections : the settled ones being village workers in cane, mat weavers and basket makers and scavengers and nomadic ones. In the south they are acrobats, dancers and bad characters generally. Prizyluski says of them that once they represented a respectable tribe and were more or less like the odumbara legendry tribe of shepherds in the Punjab.[13] In some areas their assistance is necessary at funerals to hand the wisp of lighted straw with which the chief mourner ignites the pyre.[14] Turner maintains that the hill Doms now repudiate any connection with the scavengers of the plains. They have retained a considerably higher status and something of their tribal organisation.[15] Baines divides Doms into the following groups :

1. Field labourers; 2. Weavers; 3. Metal Workers; 4. Cane workers; 5. Lower Artisans; 6. Exorcists; 7. Porters; 8. Leather workers; 9. Musicians; 10. Mendicants; and 11. Tailors.

In the Punjab there is another group of Doms slightly different in name called 'Dum' and otherwise known as 'Mirasi' who are vocationally ministers and genealogists some Jat families employing them for this purpose. They have also musical pretensions and their women give dance performances before females. Almost all of them are Muslims. In Andhra Pradesh they are known as Dombar or Dommara.[16]

The Doms are significantly large in Bengal and Uttar Pradesh. In both the regions, they are grouped among the lowest castes. Baines writes : "Here there is found a caste which if not at the bottom of the social scale, is, at least, not far from it."[17] The Doms eat all manner of unclean food. No Brahman is prepared to cater their religious needs.

As we said the Doms are traditionally concerned with scavenging. Other sub-castes of Doms are the Chuhra in the Punjab, the Bhangi and Mehtar in Rajasthan and Maharashtra the Bhunmali and Hari in Bengal and Haddi in Orissa. The Chumbra or Chuhra has been held to be the remnant of an aboriginal tribe, but in point of fact his physical type differs but little from that of other inhabitants. His outcaste position is largely due to his occupation, and when he turns Sikh, he becomes Mazhabi but even his conversion does not help him to become equal to others.[18]

The Dom leaders during my investigation in Jaunpur narrated their story that they were declared nomads and criminals during the British period. A strict watch was kept over their conduct in order to prevent them from committing further crimes. Some informed me of their origin from Satyuga when they had purchased the great king Harish Chandra. The story goes that God Vishnu in the disguise of Vishvamitra decided to test the greatness of the Maharaja Harish Chandra. Vishvamitra begged of his whole empire along with his family. And what was fuel to fire, the Maharaja's son Rohitashva was stung by a venomous snake. While his body was being lifted for funeral, the queen Taramati had no coffin to cover the bier and ultimately she tore her sari for cover. The Dom on duty, on the cremation ground was watching all this silently and did not show any sympathy. The whole tragedy occurred on account of the Dom's indifference and mercilessness. It is due to this curse that they were deprived of their good lot and had to lead a life of nomads and never getting satisfied in their life.

The Baheliyas

The Baheliyas trace their history in the Mahabharata period from Vyadh lineage of Eklavya. Eklavya was a low caste prince of non-Aryan birth in the Mahabharata period. He was the best archer of his time. Even the best archers of his time were jealous of his matchless archery. It is recorded that he was the ablest son of the king of the Nishad community. Originally they were 'hunters and fowlers'[19] but in Jaunpur from the very beginning they are quite well off and own sufficient lands. Several Baheliya youths are in service either in Calcutta or Bombay. Their strength in the population is very small, the total number being 205.

The Bansfods (Dharkars)

The Bansfods, also known as 'Dharkars, are basket makers or bamboo splitters. The Bansfods or Basors are a branch of the Dom caste. It is said about them that they will touch neither a Dom nor a Dhobi whilst the Basor extends his objection to the Musahar, Chamar, Dharkar and Bhangi.[20]

The Basors working in Bamboo have the following subcastes : (1) Dumar or Dom Basors (2) Dhubala, perhaps from the Dhobi caste (3) Dharkar.[21]

Formerly, they were a vagrant tribe, but, now they lead a settled life. They are engaged in basket making, aprons and pigeon cages. They call themselves descendants of Raja Ben.[22] The story goes that the king was illfamed for his lack of compassion towards his subjects. He had established a charitable fund of cows but gave only the crippled cows to the Brahmanas. The Brahmanas cursed him and, as a result, throughout his tenure he remained desperately dejected and restless. The Basors also suffered heavily on account of their king's plight. Since then they have been living a sub-standard life. Had the king used his discretion, they would never have been eclipsed by the freak of destiny.

The Nats

They, too, were a vagrant tribe. They are generally singers, dancers acrobats and professional criminals (the faminine is a Natni) who move about without a territorial location.[23] They are also beggars at some places and earn their living by begging. Some are cultivators. The Nat panchayats are very strict about a man's conduct and make the culprit sit in cold water for twentyfour hours. This penalty is a measure of correction and purification for the erring Nats.[24] Turner also adds that a Nat bridegroom stays and serves as long as his wife's parents are alive failing which he becomes liable for a money payment which is fixed by the caste panchayat. This custom is known as 'Ghar Jawai'. Marriage by exchange either direct or three cornered is practised among the Nats. The custom of adopting a daughter, still survives.[25] It is also a known fact that their women are associated in many parts of the country with dancing and prostitution. They are a hereditary caste of rope sliders. It is said that in former days the slider who fell off the rope was cut to pieces at bottom. The victim was hurled to the ground.[26] Nats, even today, follow their traditional pursuits.

The Kanjars

The Kanjars are recognised as stone cutters (pathar kat). They were formerly a gipsy caste of criminals or mat-makers in upper and central India. The Kanjar respondents related to me that they ran to the hills during the Mughal period in order to save themselves from the mass massacre by the Mughals. They resisted the latters' entry into the country, to their last efforts. They would invade the Mughals from behind the hills by pelting stones at them. Thus, due to continuous struggle with the Mughals, the Kanjars became homeless and vagrants and for their livehood, they had to resort to the occupation of plundering. Later, the Britishers, also, treated them as 'thugs' (dacoits) and rebels and stigmatised them as Criminals. Until the Criminal Act was repealed, they continued to be called criminals. One old respondent of this community, also, stated that they were 'Gihari Kshatriyas' of Sun lineage (Suryavamshi) who had migrated, long ago to the eastern parts of the country from the western parts.

As we have seen all the scheduled castes claim their descent from one or other mythical beings. The Bansphors connect their lineage with Raja Ben whom they regard as the first king of India. The Doms trace their descent from some great Rishi in Satyuga. The Kanjars say that they have descended from the Gihari Kshatriya class and the Baheliyas trace their origin to Ekalavya. The Khatiks, likewise, say that they have evolved as 'Sonkars'. The Musahars think that they come from Banvasi lineage. The Pasis trace their origin to Andheriya class of Kshatriya while the 'Chamars' connect them with Jai Singh and Ravana lineage.

The Scheduled Castes under study can be grouped under three broad occupational divisions (1) the agriculturists who own and cultivate the land; (2) the Craftsmen who follow certain trades; and (3) the labourers who work on daily wages. In the first group are included Pasis, Baheliyas and few Chamars. They are referred to as cultivators, or agriculturists and derive the major part of their income or subsistence from tilling their own land. In the second category are included Musahar, Bansphor, Nat, Kanjar, Khatik and Dhobis. They follow their traditional occupation with slight modification. The remaining castes—the Pasi, Dom and some Chamars eke out their livelihood from working in the fields. Their sources of origin are indicated in the Table 3.

TABLE 3

Showing Sources, Origin of Respondents

Sl. No.	*Castes*	*Agriculturists*	*Craftsmen or Trades men*	*Labourers*	*Source of origin*	*Remarks*
1.	Bansphor	—	Craftsmen	—	Raja Ben (First King of India)	
2.	Doms	—	—	Labourers	Satyugi rishi	
3.	Kanjars	—	Craftsmen	—	—	
4.	Baheliya	Agriculturists	—	—	Ekalavya	
5.	Khatiks	—	Tradesmen	—	Incognito (Now Sonkars)	
6.	Musahar	—	Craftsmen	—	Banvasi	
7.	Pasi	Agriculturists	—	Labourers	Andheriya Class Kshatriya	
8.	Chamar	Agriculturists	Craftsmen	Labourers	Jai Singh Ravan	
9.	Nat	—	Craftsmen	—	—	
10.	Dhobi	—	Craftsmen	—	—	

All the ten different castes have their own separate socio-religious identities; all of them are endogamous and exogamous groups and accept food and water at the hands of all the castes occupying a higher position in the social hierarchy. It was found during the course of study that each caste is divided into a number of sub-castes. A man's choice of a mate in his caste or sub-caste is hedged round with restrictions of endogamy and exogamy and other special rules. They observe caste endogamy strictly and the penalty for transgression of these restrictions is excommunication. Marriage outside the caste is supposed to be inconceivable. If such a thing happens, the outsider is admitted to their caste. An endogamous sub-caste is generally divided into exogamous groups. Although according to the rules of exogamy, the scheduled castes are not supposed to have any gotras, yet according to their statements it seems, they too, have their gotras such as Kachhap and Ekalavya gotras respectively. Those belonging to the Kachhap gotra do not marry themselves. The same is the case with these belonging to Eklavya gotra also. Another form of exogamy practised by the scheduled castes is the territorial village exogamy. The residents of the same village consider themselves as kins and, therefore, do not marry among themselves. Baheliyas, Bansphors (Dharkars) and Doms (Hindu) do not allow marriage in the line of the paternal aunt and maternal uncle.

Social Background of the Respondents

The respondents possess differing social, economic and cultural background and belong to diverse age group size of family and range of income. The Table 4 below shows their distribution according to their background.

TABLE 4

Showing Sex-ratio and age group of respondents

Sl. No.	*Sex*					
	Male	*Female*	*18-25 years*	*26-40 years*	*41-54 years*	*55 years and above*
1.	396/400	4/400	64/400	200/400	120/400	16/400
2.	99%	1.00%	16%	50%	30%	4%

The table above shows that out of 400 respondents, 64 (16 per cent) respondents are between the age group of 18-25 years,

200 (50 per cent), between 26-40 years 120 (30 per cent), between 41-54 years and 16 (4 per cent) between 55 years and above. 4 respondents (1 per cent) were female and 396 respondents (99 per cent) belonged to the male sex. Thus, the highest percentage of the respondents belong to the age group of 26 years to 40 years and the second highest belongs to the age group of 41 to 54 years.

Religion

The respondents belong to two religious communities, viz. Hindu and Muslims. The Hindu respondents constitute 395 (98.5 per cent) of the total and the Muslim respondents 5 (1.25 per cent) of the total respondents. No respondent belonged to any other religion. Every Hindu respondent confirmed his faith in one or other deity and firmly held that caste and religion along with their values and norms were like a 'Banyan tree' under which they safeguarded their life and survived the onslaught and danger from the outer forces. However, 4 (1.01 per cent) out of the 395 Hindu respondents expressed their feelings against caste and religion. The remaining others affirmed their loyalty to the traditional stratification of Hindu society.

Caste

In the traditional social system, caste had been a governing principle of distribution of occupations and status and of contracting

TABLE 5

Showing religion and caste of the respondents

Sl. No.	*Caste*	*Religion*		*Strength*	*%*	*Remarks*
		Hindu	*Budha*			
1.	Dom	15	5	20	5%	
2.	Chamar	140	Nil	140	35%	
3.	Khatik	30	Nil		7.50%	
4.	Pasi	30	Nil		7.50%	
5.	Nat	20	Nil		5%	
6.	Kanjar	40	Nil		10%	
7.	Dhobi	30	Nil		7.50%	
8.	Musahar	40	Nil		10%	
9.	Baheliya	10	Nil		2.50%	
10	Bansphor	40	Nil		10%	

matrimonial alliances. The following table shows distribution of the respondents, caste and religion wise :

Rural and Urban Background of the Respondents

Out of the total number of respondents 385 (96.25 per cent) come from rural areas and the remaining 15 respondents (3.75 per cent) from urban area. The table below shows the breakup of the respondents according to their place of residents :

TABLE 6

Showing the place of residence-rural/urban

Sl. No.	*Rural background*	*Urban background*
1.	385	15
2.	96.25%	3.75%

Marital Status and Nature of the Family

Of the total number of respondents 380 (95 per cent) were married, 5 (1.25 per cent) unmarried, 10 (2.50 per cent) windowers and 5 (1.25 per cent) divorcees or deserted. Out of the widower respondents 2 (20.0 per cent) were ladies who had been deserted by their husbands.

Cases under study reveal that 280 (70 per cent) respondents come from the joint-family and 120 (30 per cent) from a nuclear family. Among the married respondents (380), 152 (40 per cent) have families consisting of 1 to 3 members and 114 (30 per cent) have families consisting of 3 to 4 members and the remaining 114 (30 per cent) have families with membership of 4 to 5. The others 20 (5 per cent) have no families at all and lead a single life. Details are presented in the following Table 7.

TABLE 7

Showing marital status and nature of family

Sl. No.	*Nuclear family*	*Joint family*	*Married*	*Unmarried*	*Widows*	*Widowers*	*Divorced or deserted*	*Remarks*
1.	120/400	280/400	380/400	05/400	02/400	8/400	5/400	Nil
2.	30%	70%	95%	1.25%	0.5%	2%	1.25%	Nil

Education of the Respondents

As regard the educational attainments of the respondents, 318 (79.50 per cent) are illiterate, 3 (0.75 per cent) can read and write, 9 (2.25 per cent) are educated upto Ist standard, 12 (3 per cent) upto IInd standard, 16 (4 per cent) upto IIIrd standard, 9 (2.25 per cent) upto IVth standard, (61.5 per cent) upto Vth standard, 6 (1.50 per cent) upto VIth standard, 4 (1 per cent) upto VIIth standard, 6 (1.50 per cent) upto middle class, 1 (0.25 per cent) upto VIIIth standard, 3 (0.75 per cent) upto IXth standard, 2 (0.50 per cent) upto high school, 1 (0.25 per cent) upto intermediate, 1 (0.25 per cent) upto Sahitya Ratna, 1 (0.25 per cent) upto M.A.

Education of Grandfather and Fathers

Out of 400 respondents, only 2 (0.50 per cent) respondents' fathers and grandfathers had primary education and the remaining 398 respondent's fathers and grandfathers (99.50 per cent) had no educational background.

Income of the Respondents

(*i*) Details of the income of the respondents is presented in the table 8 below :

TABLE 8

Showing income of the respondents

Sl. No.	*Monthly income group*	*Respondents' number*	*Percentage*
1.	Between Rs. 55/- to Rs. 90/-	205	51.25%
2.	Between Rs. 91/- to Rs. 150/-	183	45.75%
3.	Between Rs. 151/- to Rs. 200/-	04	01%
4.	Between Rs. 201/- to Rs. 300/-	04	01%
5.	Between Rs. 301/- and above	04	01%

(*ii*) From the above table, it will be observed that 205 respondents (51.25 per cent) have an income of Rs. 55 to Rs. 90 per month, 183 (45.75 per cent) have an income of Rs. 91 to Rs. 150 per month and the income of the remaining 12 (3 per cent) ranges between Rs. 151 and Rs. 200 and Rs. 201 to Rs. 300 and above.

(*iii*) The average income of all the income groups comes to about Rs. 102 per month which is higher than that of the national per capita income which is Rs. 414 per annum estimated during 1964-65.

NOTES AND REFERENCES

1. Ghurye. G.S. : Caste and Class in India, Popular Book Depot Bombay, 1932, pp. 254-255.
2. Baines, A. : Ethnography (Castes and Tribes), 1932.
3. Briggs, G.W. : The Chamars, p. 13, Association Press, Calcutta, 1920.
4. Prof. P.V. Kane in 'History of Dharmshastras' mentions of Jatyatkarsha and Jatyapakarsha. In the former if a high caste Hindu marries with a low born girl and successively goes to fifth generation, the progeny in fifth generation will become Chamar. Again if it works up in another way, that is, if a low born person marries with High caste girl and successively repeats it for seven generations, the progeny in the seventh generation will, also, become a Chamar—Bhandarkar Oriental Research Institute, Poona, 1930.
5. Briggs, G.W. : The Chamars (1920) p. 21.
6. Census Report, 1891.
7. Baines, A. : *op. cit.* p. 1.
8. *Ibid.*
9. Hutton, J.H. : Caste in India, 1946 Oxford University Press p. 129.
10. Baines A : *op. cit.*, pp. 1,4.
11. (District Gazetteer of Jaunpur)—Jaunpur—A Gazetteer H.R. Nevill (1908) Govt. Press, United Province.
12. Kirkpatrick, W. : "Primitive Exogamy and the Caste System" in Proceedings A & B. Vol. No. 3, Calcutta, 1912.
13. Prizyluski : Les Udumbara. Quoted in J. H. Hutton's 'Caste in India'.
14. Baines : *op. cit.*, pp. 1,4.
15. Turner : 'Caste in the Kumaon Division and Tehri-Garhwal State, in the Report of the Census of India 1931, Vol. I, Pt. III, B. pp. 17 Sq. & Crook, Tribes Castes 11 SV Dom.
16. *Op. cit.*, pp. 1, 4, 6, 9.
17. *Ibid.*, p. 84.
18. Rose : Tribes and Castes, 11, pp. 182 Sq.
19. Crooke, W. I., pp. 45, 108, 93, 219, 326, III 274, 332 IV 33, 43 (The Tribes and Caste of the North Western Provinces and Oudh, 4 Vols. 1896).
20. U.P. Census 1911, pp. 329-331.
21. Nesfield, J.C. : 'Brief view of the caste system of the North Western Provinces & Oudh, Allahabad (1885), p. 106.

22. Srimat Bhagvat II Part. Gita Press, Gorakhpur, 1955.
23. F. Hamilton : Buchman Q. r. Edinburg, p. 55.
    Martin, M : The History of Antiquities Topography statistics of Eastern India (1838).
    Crooke, E. : *op. cit.*, pp. 11, 56.
24. O. 'Malley' L.S.S. Indian Caste, Customs, Govt. Publications.
25. Turner, A.C. : Report on the Census of United Provinces of Agra and Oudh (1931).
26. Rose : *op. cit.*, p. 11, 345 Sq.

CHAPTER FOUR

Social Organisation

Marriage

MARRIAGE DENOTES those unequivocally sanctioned unions which persist beyond sexual satisfaction and, thus, come to underlie family life.[1] There are varying practices associated with marriage in India. For, instance, the general pattern in North India is that the proposal for marriage must come from the girl's side.[2] There are, again, prohibited and preferred degrees of marriage. Endogamy and exogamy are the most common forms of marriage prevailing among the various communities in India. There are likewise restrictions on widow re-marriage.

However, marriage among the scheduled castes does not involve much complexity; it is rather a matter of convenience for both the parties. The Musahars, Kanjars, Bansphors (Dharkars), Baheliyas and Doms do not allow marriage within a man's own family, and forbid matrimonial alliances in the line of maternal aunt and maternal uncle while Chamars avoid chachera, phuphera, mamera and mausera relations. We have already referred to in the foregoing chapter that the Chamars practise exogamy also. They have their gotra divisions and avoid marriage within these divisions. No other castes except Baheliyas reported the existence of gotra divisions within it, but all including the Chamars and Baheliyas practise territorial exogamy. They do not marry within the same village.

There is, also, a general practice of exchange marriage popularly known as 'adla-badla', among some of these castes. Exchange marriage involves a simple exchange of girls between two families.

For example, A marries B's sister and B marries A's sister. This kind of marriage is generally practised by the Nats and Pasis, Musahars, Kanjars and Khatiks as well.

Marriage among the scheduled castes involves three main ceremonies : betrothal ceremony, known as 'Mangni', marriage ceremony and second marriage (gauna). If the bride has attained puberty or the groom has become adolescent, the gauna ceremony is not observed. However marriages performed at an early age begin with gauna ceremony.

However, to know their minds about the nature of matrimonial alliance, the respondents were asked, "Are you in favour of changing the existing form and procedure of marriage" ? Are you in favour of giving freedom to boys and girls to settle their own marriages ? The blanket answer that the respondents gave to the first question was 'no', that is to say, they do not want any changes to be introduced in the existing form, and procedure of marriage. Likewise, their answer to the second question was that matrimonial arrangements should rest exclusively upon the choice and consent of the parents and that no freedom, whatever need be, accorded to the boys and girls for selecting a partner for themselves. They again insist on marriage taking place within their own caste. When asked about the considerations regarding the selection of mates for their boys and girls, the respondents gave answers which are presented in the following Table 9.

TABLE 9

Showing considerations for the selection of mates for their boys and girls

Sl. No.	*Considerations*	*For boys*	*For girls*
1.	Caste	100%	100%
2.	Wealth	73%	91%
3.	Good character	59%	76%
4.	Education	75%	27%

In the above table we observe that caste is considered as an important factor in the settlement of marriage by the respondents both for boys and girls. In the case of boys education, gets the second place and in the case of girls wealth, occupies the second place. This means that next to caste, the second consideration in the marriage of boys is education while in the marriage of girls, wealth is the second. They prefer a good character girl to an educated one. But for the marriage of girls their preference centres more on the education or wealth of the boys than their good character.

Age at Marriage

Scheduled castes under study practise child-marriage. Boys are generally married between 13 years to 16 years while girls between 9 years and 11 years.[3] When the respondents were asked when did you marry ? 320 respondents (80 per cent) said that they were married at 5 to 6 years and the remaining 80 (20 per cent) at 13 to 15 years. The following Table shows the age at marriage.

TABLE 10

Showing age at marriage of respondents

Sl. No.	*Respondents*	*Percentage*	*Age at marriage*
1.	320	80%	5 to 6 years
2.	80	20%	13 to 16 years

To the second question, what changes do you like with regard to age at marriage ? 367 respondents (91.75 per cent) replied that age at marriage for boys and girls should be respectively 18 years and 14 years while the remaining 33 (8.25 per cent) pleaded for 16 years for boys and 10 years for girls. The change desired in age is indicated as follows in the Table 11.

TABLE 11

Showing desire for change in the age of marriage

Sl No.	*Respondents*	*Percentage*	*Age desired*
1.	367	91.75%	18 years for boys 14 years for girls
2.	33	8.25%	15 years for boys 10 years for girls

Thus, Table 11 shows that 91.75 per cent respondents want to raise the age of boys and girls for marriage while 8.25 per cent do not favour any change.

Widow Marriage

Re-marriage of widows and Niyoga are practised by all the scheduled castes under study. It is only the Mewafarosh Khatiks who object to it. The usual practice prevalent under Niyoga is that the widow marries her late husband's younger brother. Niyoga in this form is practised by all. But instances were also cited by the respondents where re-marriage was performed with elder brothers. However, a widow can also marry outside her husband's family. But in such cases, the new husband of the widow has to pay some compensation to the late husband's family. It was noticed in one case where the person entering into matrimonial alliance with a widow who did not belong to the husband's family and he had to pay some amount to her late husband's family.

When asked about the Hindu Widow Remarriage Act of 1956 and its validity, all the respondents except 2 (0.5 per cent) exposed their ignorance about it. The position regarding their awareness of the act is given in the following Table 12.

TABLE 12

Showing Awareness of the Remarriage Act of 1956 and its validity

Sl. No.	*Awareness*	*Respondents*	*Percentage*
1.	No knowledge of the Act	398	99.5%
2.	Knowledge of the Act and its implication	2	0.5%

Intercaste Marriage

To the question, 'Do they favour marriage outside their own caste' cent-per cent respondents answered; 'No'.

To the second question, 'What are the causes on account of which you disfavour intercaste marriages' 135 respondents (33.75 per cent) replied that their caste panchayats would penalise them and 115 respondents (28.75 per cent) advance their argument that such marriages create problems in adjustment as the partners entering into such alliance hail from diverse cultural origins while 150 (37.50 per cent) gave blanket answer that they were not mentally prepared for such adventure. The following table indicates causes which hamper intercaste marriages.

TABLE 13

Showing causes disfavouring intercaste marriage

Sl. No.	*Causes*	*Respondents*	*Percentage*
1.	Fear of disapproval and penalty by caste panchayats	135	33.75%
2.	Problem in marital adjustment	115	28.75%
3.	Not mentally prepared	150	37.50%

However, the investigator was told by the respondents during the field work about two cases of marriage with caste Hindus. One Chamar lady had married a caste Hindu which, it is said, was love marriage (Prem Vivaha). Another incident was that one Pasi woman had married a Maurya boy. Maurya is a backward caste but higher in status to the Pasis. When the respondents were asked whether they approved these marriages, their answer was that if the girl goes with a caste Hindu, it is better both for herself and her expected progeny. She will have better food, clothing and house. Moreover, her position in the community will also be elevated.

Dowry System

The custom of giving presents at the time of marriage is a universal phenomenon among all the castes in India. Dowry system has become associated with social status and family prestige and has at present introduced what might be called the prestige effect in marriages. Ordinarily, dowry is the property which a man receives from his wife's side in his marriage.[4]

To ascertain the views of the respondents about the dowry system, the respondents were asked the following questions :

(1) Do you give or accept dowry in the marriages of your sons and daughters ?

(2) Do you favour

(i) retention, or

(ii) complete abolition, or

(iii) partial abolition of the dowry system

In answer to the first question, cent per cent respondents both give and take dowry in marriages of their sons and daughters. Their responses in respect of the second question are tabulated as under :—

TABLE 14

Showing attitude of respondent towards the abolition of dowry system

Sl. No.	*Responses*	*Respondent's strength*	*Percentage*
1.	Retention of dowry favoured	340	85%
2.	Partial abolition favoured	40	10%
3.	Complete abolition favoured	20	5%

Regarding taking initiative for the abolition of dowry, 388 respondents (97 per cent) said, they are not prepared to take any initiative while 12 (3 per cent) said, they are prepared. Their responses are presented below in the Table 15.

TABLE 15

Showing responses in respect of taking initiative for abolishing dowry

Sl. No.	*Responses*	*Respondents*	*Percentage*
1.	Not prepared for any initiative	388	97%
2.	Prepared for initiative	12	3%

Asked whether they had any knowledge of the Dowry Abolition Act, 1961 and whether they welcomed the measure, the respondents said, they were not aware of it. Only one (0.25 per cent) who was

M.A. in Philosophy knew about it. Also, 228 respondents (57 per cent) did not welcome the measure while only 43 per cent welcomed it. Their reactions are shown in the Table 16.

TABLE 16

Showing reactions in respect of Dowry Abolition Bill, 1961

Sl. No.	*Reactions*	*Respondents*	*Percentage*
1.	Did not welcome the Act, 1961 as a measure	228	57%
2.	Welcomed the Act as a measure	172	43%

Dowry as an institution has late become the prestige mark of the high society in India. The system prevails among the scheduled castes also, but it is significant that they are becoming aware of its evils. The percentage that is favouring the abolition of the system is, indeed, low, but none, too significant. It does indicate that there are, at least some among the respondents who do not favour its continuance.

Divorce

Divorce implies dissolution of marriage. Marriage among the scheduled castes is cancelled when some defect such as incurable disease or physical debility is detected in the boy or the girl in the process of settling the marriages. As regards divorce after marriage, the respondents generally do not favour it. In answer to the question whether they favour divorce or not, 325 respondents (81.25 per cent) said 'no'; and 75 (18.75 per cent) said, 'yes'. Thus who said 'no' were of the view that divorce leads to 'no' enormous complexities. Those who said 'yes' were of the view that if marriage does not yield happiness, there is no point in continuing it. Their responses are Tabulated as below :

TABLE 17

Showing acceptance of divorce

Sl. No.	*Responses*	*Respondents*	*Percentage*
1.	Those who do not favour divorce	325	81.25%
2.	Those who favour divorce	75	18.75%

However, among the scheduled castes under study widow re-marriage or marriage of forsaken woman is a common practice. Divorce or desertion, therefore, does not create much problem for the women. Still the fact that majority of the respondents do not favour the idea of divorce, shows that they generally do not appreciate it. On the basis of what we have been able to say above, the following generalizations can be made with regard to marriage among it to the rise of the individualistic spirit and 8 per cent attribute it to family disputes of varying kinds such these relating to marriage, share in property and internal maladjustment. Broadly, however, the reasons are mobility individualism and family disputes.

(i) Familism is still a governing factor in the settlement of marriage among them, that none favours marriage by the mutual consent of boys and girls. To this extent that the respondents seem to be conservative in their attitude because they do not want any change.

(ii) All the castes insist on marrying their sons and daughters within their own caste. Thus, endogamy seems to be the general rule. They are against intercaste marriage but do not object to it if it takes place. In this respect, they seem to be, moreover, in its favour.

(iii) In regard to the age of marriage, again, that does seem to be a change in the attitudes of the scheduled castes. However they practise child marriage even now. Majority of the respondents favoured the raising of the age of boys and girls. Only a small percentage was of the view that no major changes were required on this direction.

Family Life

Cases under study reveal that 280 respondents (70 per cent) are from the joint family and only 120 (30 per cent) from the nuclear family. This shows that joint family is still maintaining its strangle hold among the scheduled castes. However, the remaining 30 per cent responses indicate that, a least, 1/3 families have become nuclear. This is obviously on account of the gradual break up of the joint family.

When asked as to what factors are responsible for the break up of joint family, the respondents in order of preference stated the following causes (*vide* Table 18).

TABLE 18

Showing causes for disruption of joint family

Sl. No.	*Causes*	*Number of Respondents*	*Percentage*
1.	Job mobility	297	74.25%
2.	Individualistic acquisitive spirit	71	17.75%
3.	Family disputes regarding marriage property share, distribution of roles	32	8.00%

An analysis of the table shows that 74.25 per cent respondents attribute break up of the joint family to job mobility. 17.75 per cent attribute evils.

Intercaste Relations

Johnson states that if members of two different social strata come to have intimate social relationships, there would develop among them a sense of mutual acceptability as equals or near equals. If the members of two social groups maintain social distance and interact as unequals, they would avoid and even resist social relationships with each other.[5]

The traditional pattern of social interactions between the scheduled castes and the caste Hindus reflects the idea of pollution and social distance. In order to study the extant pattern of inter-caste relations, the respondents were asked to indicate whether or not they would accept caste Hindus in certain social relations. Except for the use of drinking water wells, 340 respondents (85 per cent) are not willing to have social interactions with higher castes on the basis of equality while 60 (15 per cent) favour such relations. The responses are recorded in the Table 19.

Regarding entrance into matrimonial relations with the higher castes, cent per cent respondents expressed their unwillingness.

When asked to state the reasons of why they do not want to establish social interactions with the higher castes, 340 (85 per cent) respondents answered that they wanted to preserve their

TABLE 19

Showing responses towards acceptability of caste Hindus in social relations

Sl. No.	Responses	Respondents	Percentage
1.	Unwilling to have social relations at all	340	85%
2.	Willing to have relations except in regard to drinking water	60	15%

own identity as distinct social groups deserving special privileges presently enjoyed by them under various legislative and administrative provisions. Even contacts within scheduled castes are avoided. For instance, contact between a Chamar and a Dom is considered to be defiling. They all said that they did not practise interdining either with the caste Hindus or among themselves. More about this point further below in our discussion of social distance.[6]

Social Status

Regarding social status when asked, "Do you feel your status has improved in the Independent India ?" 234 respondents (58.5 per cent) replied that they did feel better than before and had rather developed a feeling of self assertion and had also been able to establish their own identity in social spectrum. The remainder 166 (41.5 per cent) also agreed that their position after independence had improved but they felt that they had acquired a social importance in Independent India on account of their voting rights. The Table 20 shows the improving status of the respondents.

TABLE 20

Showing status of respondents

Sl. No.	Responses	Respondents	Percentage
1.	Feeling of assertion and identity	234	58.5%
2.	Feeling of a better social status on account of voting right	166	41.5%

This point was further strengthened when the respondents were asked to indicate the impact of secular education on the scheduled castes. Cent per cent respondents answered that the influence of higher education had resulted in secularising and liberalising the attitudes of both the scheduled castes and the caste Hindus. The caste Hindus had also oriented the past values to new situations.

Social Distance

Social distance has manifested itself in form of untouchability in India. It is very difficult to trace in human history a parallel to untouchability. After independence, the speedy liquidation of untouchability has been the declared policy of the State and its practice is punishable under law. During the field work in Khetasarai, the Chamar respondents stated that they maintained social distance even amongst themselves. Even the Doms amongst them observe strict rules of pollution. A Sheikhda (a sub-caste of Dom) does not accept food at the hands of a Hela Dom, although both are the offshoots of one and the same caste.

However, the respondents told the investigator that they met together on certain social festivals; such as, Holi and in the Panchayat meetings. When the respondents represented on the Panchayat bodies or Gram Sabhas, were asked to indicate whether or not they were offered seats during the meetings of these political bodies, 3 respondents (0.75 per cent) who were, also, Pradhans replied that they were offered seats, but at distance from the caste Hindus. Smokes and drinks were, also, offered to them in earthen rather than brasswares, and the remaining 397 respondents (99.25) said that they were served food etc. in the homes of caste Hindus in the pattals made of Palash trees' leaves. The Table 21 indicates the position of untouchability as stated by the respondents.

TABLE 21

Showing responses with regard to social distance

Sl. No.	*Responses*	*No. of Respondents*	*Percentage*
1.	Seats are offered smokes and drinks are offered	03	0.75%
2.	Food served in the homes of the caste Hindus in the pattals of Palash-tree leaves	397	99.25%

Now as regards socials distance, our findings are that there is no change in the traditional practice. Democratisation has, of course, compelled the caste Hindus to relent their attitude to some extent but in their heart of hearts they still nurse the same feeling of distance. And why to single out the caste Hindus, the scheduled castes themselves continue to maintain distance as among themselves.

Temple Entry and use of Wells

The closed and simple nature of the rural society gives the various castes, ample freedom and scope to observe caste norms strictly. Traditionally, the scheduled castes were not allowed to enter the temples. There is no change in the situation even now the scheduled castes are not permitted to worship at the temples maintained by the caste Hindus. The respondents told the investigator that they could not hide their caste identity nor would they be bold enough to enter temples. 341 respondents (85.29 per cent) said that if they tried to do odd acts (act of entering temples) they would be shown their places, 59 respondents (14.75 per cent) however, said that they could have a darshan of deities in temples and offer their prayers, but from a distance.[9] The responses are indicated in the Table 22.

TABLE 22

Showing attitude of caste Hindus regarding temple entry

Sl. No.	*Responses*	*Respondents*	*Percentage*
1.	Not allowed at all	341	85.25%
2.	Allowed from a distance	59	14.75%

In the rural areas, the scheduled castes have generally got their own wells and thus carry water from their own wells. They frequently use the river ghats, canals and no upper caste has shown any indignation towards them while they have their bath.

The respondents did not mention any case of indiscrimination regarding admission to the rural and urban schools. When asked, 'Can you name the factors which motivate and promote untouchability', none answered it,

To the second question, 'whether they would like to change the caste system, they replied that human beings could not change anybody's caste'.[10]

When further asked as to why the scheduled castes do not protest against untouchability from within and from without the caste, cent per cent respondents did try to raise their voices against this evil practice. Since they were themselves economically dependant on others, nobody would care to listen to them.[11]

To the next query whether legislation, education and economic independence would liquidate untouchability ? The answers given by the respondents are given in the Table 23.

TABLE 23

Showing responses regarding the abolition of untouchability

Sl. No.	*Responses*	*Respondents*	*Percentage*
1.	Legislation would liquidate untouchability	51	12.75%
2.	Education would liquidate it	138	34.50%
3.	Economic independence would liquidate it	211	52.75%

The above table shows that the majority of the respondents are of the view that their economic independence by which they obviously mean a better economic and social status is the best method of liquidating untouchability. The next best is education and the third is social legislation.

When asked to indicate whether or not they are served by the barbers and washermen, 20 Dom (5 per cent) respondents said that the washermen were not serving them, but barbers were. In rural areas the scheduled castes have their own castemen who serve them.

To the question, 'whether the priests go to their places for supervising ceremonies, etc., cent per cent informants stated that they visited their houses on request and also supervised their rituals stealthily and accepted their fees, but did not take meals at their places.' In lieu of meals, they accepted flour, pulses, money and clothes from them.

To conclude, untouchability and social distance are still practised by the scheduled castes as well as higher castes. The only change that has come about is that the scheduled caste members are now offered seats and served with drinks in the village Panchayat meetings, but as we have found that they are expected, even now, to sit at a distance from the caste Hindus. However, none of the scheduled castes mentioned about any indiscrimination regarding admission to the rural and urban schools.

Begar

Begar or forced labour has been abolished under article 23 of the Constitution (Fundamental Rights). No practice of begar[11a] was observed during the Field work, but 'Harwahi Pratha' engaging scheduled caste for menial work such as, tilling of land and looking after cattle on monthly or annual payment or for repayment of old debts, still, exists. (10 per cent) 14 Chamar respondents out of 140 reported that whenever they took loans from the land owner, one member of their family had to work for the creditor in lieu of the loan till the money was repaid.

Reference Group

In order to study the aspirations of the scheduled castes an attempt was made to analyse their reference group behaviour. Writing about reference group, Merton says : that men act in a social frame of reference, yielded by groups of which they are a part is a notion undoubtedly ancient and probably sound. There is, however, the further fact that men frequently orient themselves to groups other than their own in shaping their behaviour and evaluations.[12] Reference group according to Merton—involves three processes :

1. There is a reference group of imitation whose ways of behaviour are accepted as right and proper as useful and, therefore, to be imitated.[13]
2. There is a reference group of identification to which an individual refers when identifying himself.
3. There is a negative reference group which stand as one's enemy.

We found that 359 (89.75 per cent) respondents identified themselves with Kshatriya and 41 (10.25 per cent) with Brahmans.

The Table 24 below indicates the identification ground of the respondents.

TABLE 24

Showing identification groups of scheduled caste respondents

Sl. No.	*Identification group*	*Respondents*	*Percentage*
1.	Identification with Kshatriyas	350	89.75%
2.	Identification with Brahmans	41	10.25%

We also found that 65 respondents (16.25 per cent) had stated that they were observing the upanayan, a ritual followed by Brahmans, moustache style of dress of Kshatriyas while 335 (83.75 per cent) were also on the way to Sanskritization. When asked to indicate whether they considered the upper case Hindus as their reference group or the westernized Indians. 347 (86.75 per cent) respondents said their reference group was westernized classes while 53 (13 55 per cent) said that their model of imitation was the upper caste Hindus.

TABLE 25

Showing the Reference Group of respondents

Sl. No.	*Reference group*	*Respondents*	*Percentage*
1.	Westernized Indians	347	86.75%
2.	Upper caste Hindus	53	13.25%

When asked as to why they prefer westernization or Sanskritization, 322 respondents (80.5 per cent) stated that because westernization stood for secularism and a higher life and conspicuous consumption whereas 25 (6.25 per cent) said that it gave freedom and opportunity for mobility to them. Those who favoured Sanskritization 53 (13.25 per cent) said that their love for Sanskritization was on account of their allegiance to the regional surroundings and simple living. Their responses are presented in the Table 26.

TABLE 26

Showing the reason for acceptance of Sanskritization and Westernization

Sl. No.	*Reasons for acceptance*	*Respondents*	*Percentage*
1.	Westernization stands for secularism higher standard of life and conspicuous consumption	322	80.50%
2.	Westernization gives freedom and opportunity for mobility	25	6.25%
3.	Sanskritization stands for Indian values, simple living	53	13.25%

Attitude Towards Clubs and Association

Membership of different associations indicates social participation in community life, it also gives opportunity for relaxation expression, protection and occupational interest.

Among the respondents none has evinced any eagerness to organise any sort of organisation or recreational association. Even the Community Development blocks have not shown any interest in giving orderly structure to their scheme of Yuvak Mangal Dal. However, 12.3 per cent out of 400 respondents were members of Co-operative Society which was running under the supervision of the block in the Kerakat Tehsil. They told the investigator that though not recreation-oriented, the society was helpful to them in giving loans on cheap rates of interest.

Attitude Towards Traditional Values

It was also discovered during the investigation that the respondents had full faith in traditional values or in other words they did not want to change their traditional way of life. Every institution and group to which they belong has a distinct structure and well defined objective and expectation. They, therefore, did not like to do any thing which might undermine their loyalty to these institutions and groups. Deviation from traditionalism in other words meant to them deprivation of many good things. They therefore, pleaded its retention till their blood and life. They believed that the traditional institutions provided them cover conditions against displacement and psychological maladjustment and strains. Also they felt that tradition could neither be neglected nor overlooked because they were the repository of wisdom, experience as well as ideals of the community. When questioned closely some of them did admit that tradition obstructed progress and suppressed free-will.

As the fact stands the scheduled castes do not like to discontinue with traditions even though some of them do feel that they are obstacles to progress.

Attitude Towards Fatalism

As whether the lot of the man was predestined or could be made by one's own efforts, 360 respondents (90 per cent) said that the lot of man was predestined, only 25 (6.25 per cent) said that it could be changed by efforts. 15 respondents (3.75 per cent) felt that even man's lot was fixed but it could be altered by sheer personal endeavour. Below, Table 27 shows the responses :

TABLE 27

Showing fatalism of respondents

Sl. No.	*Responses*	*Respondents*	*Percentage*
1.	Lot predestined	360	90%
2.	Lot can be changed	25	6 25%
3.	Lot fixed but can be altered	15	3.75%

Attitude Towards Community Life

Among 400 repondents 240 (60 per cent) said that they were not fairly respresented in the local bodies, while 160 (40 per cent) admitted that they had better representation in the local organisation, such as Gaon Sabha, Nyaya Panchayats. Three respondents (0.75 per cent) were holding the membership of the Gaon Sabha and 1 (0.25 per cent) was the member of Nyaya Panchayat. When they were asked to give reasons for their small representation, they frankly confessed their own faults. Firstly, they said, they were less organised, secondly, they were less educated and thirdly they were psychologically awestricken by the Hindu caste order.[14]

Below Table 28 presents the representation of scheduled castes in the local bodies and reasons for small representation.

TABLE 28

Showing representation in local bodies

Sl. No.	*Representation in*	*Respondents*	*Percentage*
1.	Better representation in local bodies	160	40%
2.	Holding membership in local bodies	3	75%
3.	In Nyaya Panchayat	1	25%

Attainment of Higher Status by Giving up of Unclean Activities and Habits

322 respondents (80.5 per cent) admitted that they could attain the upper stratum of society only if they were prepared to give up liquor, beef eating and other unhealthy habits. But 78 respondents (19.5 per cent) help the view that avoiding of the said indulgence would make no difference at all. It was rather folly to cherish such a notion because the upper castes were also indulging in them and yet continued to enjoy status in society.[15]

Attitude Towards Movies

One respondent (1.75 per cent) disclosed that they saw films weekly, 53 (13.25 per cent) said they saw them monthly while

TABLE 29

Showing visits to Movies

Sl. No.	*Visits*	*Respondents*	*Percentage*
1.	Weekly visit to movies	07	1.75%
2.	Monthly visit	53	13.25%
3.	Once a year	340	85%

340 (85 per cent) reported that since they had no extra money they could not go to movies even once a year. They had a good opinion about the impact of films. They admitted in good faith that films

had been rendering great service, and to a great extent, helped in the eradication of social values while 20 respondents (5 per cent) adopted a neutral attitude. The Table 30 indicates visits to movies.

Attitude Towards being called Harijan

Only 26 respondents (6.5 per cent) out of 400 preferred to be called scheduled castes, 370 (92.5 per cent) saying that they would prefer being named Harijan, 4 respondents (1 per cent) wanted complete deletion of the term 'Harijan' although all the respondents welcoming these confessed that by being called 'Harijans' they had secured a number of benefits. They appreciated the Govt. measures taken by it for the amelioration of their social and economic conditions. The Table 30 below indicates the attitude of respondents towards Harijan calling :

TABLE 30

Showing attitude towards being called Harijans

Sl. No.	*Attitude*	*Respondents*	*Percentage*
1.	Prefer to be called scheduled castes	26	6.5%
2.	Prefer to be called Harijan	370	92.5%
3.	Prefer complete deletion of Harijan word	4	1%

Attitude Towards Religion

In order to ascertain the respondents' attitude towards religion, the following questions were addressed :

1. Do you believe in God ?
2. Do you join the prayers in the temple everyday or Pray at your home ?
3. Do you get mental consolation or spiritual peace by visiting the places of worship ?

In answer to the first question, cent per cent respondents believed in God. Responses in respect of the second question were that 396 respondents (99 per cent) visited the places of worship occasionally while 4 informants (1 per cent) visited these places regularly. Their responses are tabulated as follows.

TABLE 31

Showing distribution of respondents visiting the place of worship

Sl. No.	*Responses*	*Respondents*	*Percentage*
1.	Visit the places of worship occasionally	396	99%
2.	Visit the places of worship regularly	4	1%

Regarding the third question, cent per cent respondents replied that visiting the places of worship had both mental consolation and spiritual peace for them.

NOTES AND REFERENCES

1. Lowie, Robert H. : Marriage in Encyclopaedia of Social Sciences, Vol. X, p. 146.
2. Ibbetson, Denzil (1880). The Races, Castes and Tribes of the People (reprint) in the Report of the Census of the Punjab Published in 1883.
3. Bernard, Cohn S. : 'The Chamars of Senapur (1954) unpublished Ph.D. dissertation also cites age of marriage among the Chamars ranging between 13 years and 16 years (boys) and 10 years (girls).
4. Winick Charles defines dowry constituting those valuables that the relatives of either party in a marriage contribute—Dictionary of Anthropology, p. 174.

   Kamla Devi Chattopadhyaya in her article 'Is the Dowry System Desirable?' in the *Illustrated Weekly of India,* December 2, 1956 accepts it as a legal entity.
5. Henry M. Johnsons : Sociology—A Systematic Introduction (Indian Edition), 1966, Bombay Allied Publishers, p. 504.
6. A. Gogegamage & P.V. Veeraraghavan in their work 'Status Images in Changing India', (Bombay, Manaktala 1967) also indicates that the untouchables enjoy lower acceptability as compared to other castes.

   H.S. Bhatia also in his article, Intercaste relations and Aspirational levels—An Attitude study appeared in Indian Journal of Social Work, Vol. XXXI No. 1, April 1970, says that the Harijans do not seem to be willing to have special interactions on equality basis in any great measure.
7. Aiyappan, A. in Social Revolution in a Kerala Village—A Study in Cultural Change (1965) The Irvas, An Untouchable Caste in Kerala, (Bombay) maintains that with greater awareness of their Political significance and the emergence of vested interests within these communities, this tendency is likely to become more apparent.

8. A.L. Srivastava in his article 'Attitude Towards Harijans Yet to Change Social Welfare', October, 1970, p. 11 states that more often the feeling has gone to the extent of arrogance and rebellion against caste Hindus.

9. Taya Zinkin 'In A Tanjore Village' remarks that in a Tanjore village, the Harijan himself would probably not try to enter a caste shrine and if he did, the village castes would probably soon bring him to heel, law or no law.

10. Dube, S.C. in 'Indian Villages', p. 224, Routledge and Kegan Paul 1965, remarks that the untouchables are careful not to voice their protest too publicly for they are conscious of the advantage of silence in view of their dependant position in the economic structure of community.

(ii) Srinivas, M.N. in his study 'Caste In Modern India & Other Essays (p. 104) observes as long as the Harijans are not economically independent, of the high castes, the rights which the constitution guarantees will not be translated into practice.

11. Ninth Report of the Commissioner for Scheduled Castes says that untouchability in U.P., Rajasthan (51 villages covered) Gujarat and Maharashtra varies considerably from village to village and the intolerant practices are waning fast. Cases of indiscrimination are rare.

11a. Bonded labour or Jeetha System among scheduled castes still exists in rural areas of Karnataka. Usha Rao : Deprived Castes in India, 1981.

An all India survey conducted by the All India Harijan Sewak Sangh reveals in twelve states that the prevalence of untouchability still continues

Sl. No.	*Name of State*	*No. of Villages Surveyed*	*No entry in temples, hotels, wells— Numbers*	*Service of Barbars and washermen denied*
1.	Andhra Pradesh	60	17,16,14 villages	48 & 18
2.	Gujarat	141	89,130,126 villages	130
3.	Himachal Pradesh	51	49	—
4.	Karnataka	100	In all 100 villages	In all
5.	Kerala	68	68	—
6.	Maharashtra	61	29,26 & 4	17 villages
7.	Madhya Pradesh	199	92,95 villages	145 127 villages
8.	Haryana	44	In 23 villages	—
9.	Tamil Nadu	148	115,136 & 36 villages	—
10.	U.P.	170	55,87 & 113 villages	63 villages

12. Merton Robert, K. Social Theory and Social Structure, Glencoe : The Free Press, 1957.

13. This is similar to Turner's reference group of identification (Turner, Ralph, H.: in Role taking, Role stand point & Reference Group Behaviour, American Journal of Sociology (1956) p. 328.

14. Srinivas, M.N. in his Social Change in Modern India (p. 6) in 1962 modified his hypothesis of Sanskritization by the statement that Sanskritization is a process by which a lower Hindu caste or tribal or other group changes its customs, ritual and ideology and way of life in the direction of the dominant caste of a region.

15. Srinivas further refers to westernization as process involving the acceptance of western dress, diet, manners, education, gadgets, sports, values and so forth.

    Weber Bernand describes in Social stratification (1957) Harcourt Braneo and Co. New York dage 404 westernization as a change in the system of Symbolic justification and not in the system of Social Structure.

CHAPTER FIVE

Occupational Mobility

IN THE PREVIOUS CHAPTERS we tried to analyse the changing social attitudes and aspirations of the scheduled castes. In what follows, an attempt is made to examine the trend of social mobility among them. Social mobility is a term of wide connotation; it refers both to vertical and horizontal movement of people from one class or stratum to another and from one occupation or profession to another. There is extensive literature on the subject of social mobility which it would not be necessary to review at this place. For the purpose of this enquiry we have taken only occupational changes in the life of the scheduled castes in three generations, we limited our study to occupational mobility for two main reasons: one with the universe that we had before us, it was hardly possible to show conclusively whether vertical social mobility has taken place among the scheduled castes,[1] and two, occupational mobility indicates among other things whether a particular group or section of population is engaged in primary, secondary or tertiary occupation which is a positive index of development.[2] For it is accepted on all hands that shift of population from primary agricultural occupations is a positive sign of industrialization and urban growth. So, by analysing occupational mobility among our respondents we have been able to show how far they, have changed from their grandfathers' generation and what do the changes if any indicates. It is well known that in the caste society of India occupations were hereditary. As late as in the 19th century, Ghurye observed that there was no freedom of occupation among a larger number of

TABLE 32

Showing occupations of grandfathers

Sl. No.	*Caste*	*Respondents*	*Percentage*	*Occupation*
1.	Chamar	$\frac{140}{400}$	35%	Agricultural labour
2.	Dom	$\frac{20}{400}$	5%	Scavenging
3.	Khatik	$\frac{30}{400}$	7.5%	Vegetable Fruit selling and Piggery
4.	Nat	$\frac{20}{400}$	5%	Begging and Acrobatics
5.	Pasi	$\frac{30}{400}$	7.5%	Agricultural labour and Piggery
6.	Dhobi	$\frac{30}{400}$	7.5%	Washing
7.	Kanjar	$\frac{40}{400}$	10%	Stone cutting
8.	Bansphor	$\frac{40}{400}$	10%	Basket making
9.	Musahar	$\frac{40}{400}$	10%	Dona pattal making
10.	Baheliya	$\frac{10}{400}$	2.5%	Agriculture

castes.[8] The position since then has changed considerably ; but let us see what our own findings in this respect are. Above is given the Table showing the occupation of respondents generation-wise. Table 32 shows the occupation of the respondents' grandfathers.

It is evident from the table that 140 Chamar respondents' grandfathers (35 per cent) were agricultural labourers, 20 Dom respondents' grandfathers were scavengers, 30 Khatik respondent's grandfathers were vegetables growers, fruit sellers and pig husbanders, 20 Nat respondents' grandfathers were beggars and acrobats,

30 Dhobi respondents' grandfathers were Washermen, 40 Musahar respondents' grandfathers were Dona makers for marriage and confectioners, 40 Bansphors' grandfathers were basket and apron makers, 40 Kanjar respondents' grandfathers were stone-cutters (formerly they were thugs), 10 Baheliya respondents' grandfathers were agriculturists (formerely they were fowlers` and 30 Pasi respondents' grandfathers were pig husbanders and agriculturists.

On the basis of the above analysis, it can be inferred that 42.5 per cent of the respondents' grandfathers may be included in the category of agricultural labourers with no special skill or qualification (35 per cent Chamars and 7.5 per cent Pasis) and Baheliya 2.5 per cent and Khatik 7.5 per cent totalling 10 per cent respondents' grandfathers may be put in the category of agriculturists and the remaining 47.5 per cent respondents' grandfathers may be placed in the category of craftsmen and tradesmen.

Occupation of Fathers

Table 33 indicates below the occupations of the respondents' fathers :

TABLE 33

Showing occupations of fathers

Sl. No.	*Chamar*	*Baheliya*	*Other castes*
1.	14/140 (10%)	10 (2.5%)	Did not indicate any change at all
2.	Tannery	Agriculture	

Coming to father's generation, we find that 14 out of 140 (10 per cent) Chamars respondent's fathers had changed their paternal occupations and adopted tanning. Likewise the 10 Baheliya (2.5 per cent of total lot of respondents) respondents' fathers had also forsaken their parental occupations. Other castes did not show any change. In father's generation we, therefore, notice that people had started moving from their parental to other occupations or in other words from dependant occupation of agricultural labours to independent occupations such as trades like tanning of leather.

Occupation of Respondents

Occupations of the respondents are tabulated as under in the Table 34.

TABLE 34

Showing occupations of respondents

Sl. No.	*Castes*		*Occupations of respondents*
1.	Chamar	140/400	Shoe-making (35), cobblery (25), Agricultural labour (16), Masonry (4), Rickshaw Pulling(12) Tanners (8), Car driving (1), Govt. service (26), Agriculture (4)
2.	Dom	20/400	Scavenging (18), Clinic job in the Hospital (1), Rickshaw pulling (1)
3.	Khatik	30/400	Piggery (12), Vegetable growing (10), Fruit selling (4), Business in Bullocks (4)
4.	Pasi	30/400	Pig husbandry (9), Muneemgiri (1), Carpentary (1), Agriculture (8), Agricultural labour (10), Tonga driving (1)
5.	Nat	20/400	Begging (8), Acrobatics (11) and Palladari (1)
6.	Kanjar	40/400	Stone cutting (40) & dressing of flour chakkies
7.	Dhobi	30/400	Laundry (5), Washing of clothes through traditional method (25)
8.	Musahar	40/400	Dona pattal making (36), Water carrying (1), Labour in the market (on daily wages) (3)
9.	Baheliya	10/400	Government service (in factory at Calcutta) (2), Agriculture (8)
10.	Bansphor	40/400	Government service (Railways) (1), Basket making (39)

We can infer from Table 34 that in the respondents' generation, Chamars are going in larger numbers for jobs other than their parental ones. The caste occupations of the respondents in other castes, such as, Dom, Khatik, Pasi, Nat, Dhobi, Baheliya and Bansphors are slowly disappearing in the third generation. But the Kanjars have not shown any change. 35 Chamar respondents have shifted from their traditional occupation to shoe-making, 25 to cobblery 4 to masonry, 21 to rickshaw pulling, 1 to car driving, 26 have joined government service and 4 are now engaged in agriculture. In total 116 Chamar respondents have changed their father's occupation. Only 8 Chamar respondents are now engaged in their father's occupation of tanning and 16 are working as field labourers or harwahas. From among Dom respondents only 2 respondents have left their fathers' job and have taken to clinic job and rickshaw pulling while 18 are still doing their hereditary occupation. In case of Khatiks, only 4 respondents left their fathers' job and have taken to the business of bullock selling, an independent and lucrative occupation. 1 Pasi respondent has taken to muneemgiri and 1 to carpentry, 1 to tonga driving and 8 to agriculture, the remaining Pasis are carrying out their paternal occupation. Only 1 Nat has changed his father's occupation and taken to palladari. The Kanjar respondents have not shown any change even in their third generation. Of course, 5 Dhobi respondents have opened their own laundry in the towns. From among the Musahar respondents only 1 respondent has left his parental job and 3 respondents started to earn daily wages by manual labour in the market while their neighbouring Bansphors are still doing their fathers' occupation, but one is doing service in railway department, at Calcutta. Thus, out of 400 respondents we find that 147 (36.75 per cent) have changed their occupations in the third generation. This leads to the conclusion that out of every 100 respondents 9.19 per cent persons have given up their parental occupations.

It is equally important to note here that the respondents in the third generation are losing their attraction for agriculture labour and traditional occupations, although the Kanjar respondents numbering 40 (10 per cent) of the total respondents are still carrying on their traditional occupation of dressing flour chakkies and stone cutting.

The sudden but slow emergence of 30 (7.5 per cent) respondents as government servants point to the growing consciousness for white collar jobs among the respondents. Even though departure from the caste based occupation is itself no indication of an upward movement in the social scale, yet from the data in hand, it can be safely inferred that there is a slow but steady movement from dependant unskilled occupation to independent ones. This is, undoubtedly, a sign of development, howsoever, insignificant it may be.

TABLE 35

Showing inter-generational mobility in occupation

Grandfathers' generation	*Fathers' generation*	*Respondents' generation*		
All were carrying out their traditional occupations as indicated in Table 32	14 Chamars adopted Tanning as given in Table 33	Rickshaw Pulling	—	22
		Shoe-making	—	35
		Cobblery	—	25
		Masonry	—	4
		Clinical job	—	1
		Car driving	—	1
		Govt. service	—	30
		Laundry	—	5
	10 Baheliyas had already forsaken their occupation even before their grandfathers	Palladari	—	1
		Water carrying	—	1
		Muneemgiri	—	1
		Business in bullocks	—	1
		Carpentry	—	1
		Agriculture	—	12
		Labour in the market (on daily wages)	—	3
		Tonga driving	—	1
		Total	—	147
		Traditional occupations	—	253

We can, therefore, now generalize that :

1. there is slow spatial mobility from rural areas to urban areas in search of service.
2. the respondents have shown preference for independent secondary occupations over primary dependant occupations.

3. the respondents are no longer attracted towards agricultural labour.
4. the interest in white collar job is becoming slowly apparent.
5. there was a common belief in the grandfathers' generation and also in the fathers' generation that people with an agricultural occupation were the best of all. This belief is now diminishing as the Tables 34 & 35 indicate. In fathers' generation only 15 Chamars gave up their paternal jobs but in the respondents gereration 147 respondents have changed their fathers' occupations.
6. The total picture of the inter-generational mobility among the respondents can be seen from the Table 35.

Attitude Towards Fathers' Job

The data at hand reveal that 253 respondents (63 25 per cent) desire to hug to the traditional occupations because they are neither equipped to obtain jobs other than their own nor they like to move to far off places leaving their families, behind alone. 147 (36.75 per cent) respondents dislike their fathers' jobs as these jobs neither provide better emoluments nor fetch any reputation to them.

The following Table 36 indicates the attitude of respondents towards their fathers' occupation :

TABLE 36

Showing distribution of attitude of respondents regarding occupations of fathers

Sl. No.	*Responses*	*Respondents*	*Percentage*
1.	Like their fathers' occupation	253	63.25%
2.	Dislike their fathers' occupation	147	36.75%

Attitude to Present Occupation

When asked to indicate whether the respondents were satisfied with their present job, 300 respondents (75 per cent) said that they were satisfied with the present job not because they really liked it but because they could not get better jobs on account of their lack of education and skill while 100 respondents (25 per cent) adopted a neutral outlook about their job. Table 37 indicates their responses as under :

TABLE 37

Showing attitude towards present job

Sl. No.	*Responses*	*Respondents*	*Percentage*
1.	Satisfied with the present job	300	75%
2.	Adopted a neutral outlook	100	25%

Desire for Change

To the question, 'Do you have any desire to change the present job, 133 respondents (33 25 per cent) indicated their desire for change, 42 respondents (10.5 per cent) did not show any sign of change while 225 respondents (56.25 per cent) longed for better conditions and facilities,[4] The position is as follows in the Table 38.

TABLE 38

Showing desire for change in present occupation

Sl. No.	*Responses*	*Respondents*	*Percentage*
1.	Desired change	133	33.25%
2.	Neutral	42	10.50%
3.	Longed for improvement in the present job	225	56.25%

Attitude Towards Work Conditions

When asked to indicate whether the present work is satisfactory or unsatisfactory, 135 respondents (33.75 per cent) thought that the condition of their work was good and satisfactory while 265 respondents (66.25 per cent) considered that the work condition in their occupations were unsatisfactory. Details are shown in the Table 39,

TABLE 39

Showing attitude towards work conditions

Sl. No.	*Responses*	*Respondents*	*Percentage*
1.	Satisfactory	135	33.75%
2.	Unsatisfactory	265	66.25%

Source of Present jobs other than their Fathers

To the question, 'How did you get in service, 30 respondents said that they were helped in getting in their new jobs by employment exchange in the district, 18 (4.5 per cent) respondents get their jobs through competition while 99 (24.75 per cent) got their jobs through demand and supply in the market or some intermediary and the remaining 253 (63.25 per cent) had not to go anywhere else, but got their occupations from their families. The position is shown in the following Table 40.

TABLE 40

Showing sources of employment in the present job

Sl. No.	*Sources of employment*	*Respondents*	*Percentage*
1.	Through employment Exchange	30	7.5%
2.	Through Competition	18	4.5%
3.	Through demand and supply in the market	99	24.75%
4.	Inherited from parents	253	63.25%

Occupational Mobility in the Present Generation

To the question, 'How many times did you change your occupations in your life, 29 (7.25 per cent) respondents in government service indicated that they did not change their occupation since they were appointed, 5 respondents (1.25 per cent) changed twice, 13 respondents (3.25 per cent) changed thrice and the remaining 100 respondents (25 per cent) changed four times within a span of four years. This means that the respondents do have the urge to get into better jobs and are willing to change their present jobs for better ones. The change of occupation is shown in the Table 41.

TABLE 41

Showing occupational mobility of those who shifted to new occupations from the traditional ones

Sl. No.	Change in service	Respondents	Percentage
1.	No Change	29	7.25%
2.	Changed twice	5	1.25%
3.	Changed thrice	13	3.25%
4.	Changed four times	100	25%
5.	Static	253	63.25%

Attitude Towards Factors Leading to Promotion

Both internal and external forces are responsible for mobility in the traditional occupational structure. The external forces include land legislation, secular ideas regarding social matter, industrialisation, urban contacts, roads and education etc. The internal forces are hard work, faithful observance of duty and luck. However, both types of forces of occupational mobility are inter-related and operate in a cumulative way. Both the forces at the same time have both psychological and sociological implications : aspirations for higher occupational grades, better standard of living and non-manual work may be considered psychological and aspiration for status, either by adopting or discarding certain occupations may be regarded as sociological. When asked to answer the question : 'Do you take success in life to be the product of hard work, luck or otherwise ? 350 respondents (87.5 per cent) out of 400 replied that faithful observance of duty played a very important role in ones promotion, 18 (4.5 per cent) respondents remained neutral or either of the factors while 32 (8 per cent) indicated that luck determined the chances of promotion. The responses are tabulated as under in the Table 42.

TABLE 42

Showing factors responsible for success in life

Sl. No.	Factors	Respondents	Percentage
1.	Hard work	350	87.5%
2.	Luck	32	8%
3.	Neutral	18	4.5%

Social Outlook

Regarding the question of social outlook, and its role in success, 81 respondents (20.25 per cent) stood for the social outlook as responsible for promotion, 19 respondents (4.75 per cent) considered that the influence of relatives in better places of employment decided the chances of their service and promotion, 183 (45.75 per cent) respondents said that educational training helped more in getting good jobs and facilitating further promotion while 117 (29.25 per cent) maintained that it was only God who fixed the luck of man and thus, the acquisition of good service was entirely in his hands. Responses are reproduced in Table 43 as under :

TABLE 43

Showing view regarding factors (social outlook) responsible for success

Sl. No.	*Responses*	*Respondents*	*Percentage*
1.	Social outlook	81	20.25%
2.	Educational training	183	45.75%
3.	Influence of relatives	19	4.75%
4.	Heaven	117	29.25%

Aspiration for Class and Status

Economic backwardness and psychological frustration[6] also affect occupational mobility. Members of some castes who felt that their social status was inferior on account of the inferior grades of their occupations had a tendency to discard their occupations : Chamars are one of these. Our study shows that at least 29 out of 140 Chamars have given up tanning and taken to service. Tanning is undoubtedly an independent occupation and more lucrative than service. But the Chamar respondents told me that since it was an unclean pursuit which affected their status, they have given it up for lucrative, a less but socially more desirable occupation. During the investigation it was discovered that 2 respondents (0.5 per cent) longed for upper class, 100 respondents (25 per cent) aspired for middle class while the remaining 238 respondents (74.5 per cent) did not indicate their aspiration for identification with any class. One point of considerable significance is that the respondents have given subjective answer to the question, 'To which social class do you think to belong' ? Their answers seem to have been influenced by numerous considerations, such as notion of prestige, the staus of the family, caste and the income. Their aspirations are shown as below in Table 44.

TABLE 44

Showing aspiration for class

Sl. No.	*Aspiration*	*Respondents*	*Percentage*
1.	Upper class	2	0.5%
2.	Middle class	100	25%
3.	No class indicated	298	74.5%

Sub-Urban Rural Difference and Occupational Mobility

Occupational mobility is sometimes affected also by the economic structure of the village community. The village cannot provide sufficient and suitable job opportunities to all the village people. Secondly, there is no easy access to any urban centre for seeking employment. Consequently people are forced to go out of the village to earn their livelihood. The structure of village community, therefore, encourages both migration and education. 30 respondents (7.5 per cent) under study who have joined government service preferred migrate to outer places for they could not live without meals in the village.

Aspiration for Children's Job

So far we have been concerned with the inflow analysis of occupational mobility, we tried to show how the respondents have changed their occupation from their grandfathers' generation. For an outflow analysis i.e. to find out what the aspirations of the respondents towards their children's occupations, are we asked them the following questions. Which of the following jobs would you like your children to adopt ?

1. Engineering. 2. Medical profession. 3. Police job. 4. PSC jobs 5. Legal profession. 6. Military jobs. 7. Railway service. 8. Agriculture. 9. Business. 10. Political Post. 11. Choice of children themselves.

170 respondents (42.5 per cent) liked their children to go for engineering, 60 respondents (15 per cent) wanted to see that their children were in the medical line as doctors, 25 respondents (6.25 per cent) wished their children to become Police inspectors. 45 respondents (11.25 per cent) made a point to get their children recruited in the PCS cadre, 14 respondents (3.5 per cent) longed for their children to follow their traditional occupation (agriculture), 7 respondents (1.75 per cent) wanted their sons to enter into business and 4 respondents (1 per cent) desired that their sons might start as leaders in legislative bodies or parliament, 30 respondents (7.5 per cent) preferred the legal profession and 2 respondents (0.5 per cent) liked military jobs as the best career while 23 respondents (5.75 per cent) preferred railway service for their children. The remaining 20 respondents (5 per cent) gave no clear answers to the query and only liked their children to choose any job they would prefer. The Table 45 indicates the aspiration of the respondents for their children.

TABLE 45

Showing aspirations for children's job

Sl. No.	*Job preferred for children*	*Respondents*	*Percentage*
1.	Engineering	170	42.5%
2.	Medical profession	60	15%
3.	Police job	25	6.25%
4.	Public service commission	45	11.25%
5.	Legal profession	30	7.75%
6.	Military job	2	0.5%
7.	Railway service	23	5.75%
8.	Agriculture	14	3.5%
9.	Business	7	1.75%
10.	Legislative/M.P.	4	1%
11.	Choice by children	20	5%

From the Table 45 it can be inferred that the respondents, in majority favour the career of an engineer. Other occupations in the decreasing order of preference are medical profession, administrative service, railway service, agriculture, legislators/M.P. and military service. The following generalizations can be made on the basis of the facts shown in the Table 45 with regard to the aspiration of respondents for their children's job that :

1. Primary occupations do not have much charm for the respondents at present.

2. Respondents have shown their preference for Engineering and medical profession on account of their remunerative value.

3. The respondents have not shown any desire for undertaking an industrial enterprise. Only 7 respondents (1.75 per cent) wanted to go in for petty trades and business.

4. No respondent has indicated his liking for any creative work or teaching profession.

5. Respondents feel the impact of urbanization and accept that the present change in their attitudes is on account of their frequent contact with the urban people and governmental agencies who approach them often. Their proximity to such influences has been furthered by the rapid expansion of means of transport and communication.

NOTES AND REFERENCES

1. P.A. Sorokin in Social and Cultural Mobility (1959) page 11 observes that mobility as a social phenomena refers to change or alteration in status of an individual or a group. In fact, it indicates upward or downward changes in the economic, political or occupational status of either the individual or a whole group.

2. Miller, S.M. in Comparative Social Mobility, p. 5 has dilated, in details, the inter-generational mobility which indicates changes in the individual's occupational position during his life time—Current Sociology, Vol. IX No. 1 (1960) p. 5.

3. Ghurye, G.S. in Caste and Occupation (1961) Popular Book Depot, Bombay, p. 241 states the unfreedom of occupation in actual operation at the beginning of the 19th century was accompanied by a staunch belief that almost everyone of large number of castes had an occupation which was its own traditional and hence the hereditary occupation of its members to which in search of another was at least not proper, if not actually sinful.

4. B.K. Roy Burman in Social Mobility Movements among Scheduled Castes and Tribes of India, Govt. of India Press, New Delhi-11 observes that change of occupation has been reported in respect of 13 Scheduled Castes from all over India :

State/District	*Caste*	*Traditional work*	
A. Rajasthan (Kota)	Bairwa	Leather work	Change in occupation left handling the carcass of cattle and making shoes.
B. Rajasthan (Bhilwada)	Bhambi	Leather work	Taken up agriculture along with leather work.
C. Rajasthan (Sikar)	Balai	Cotton weaving and leather work	Left-leather work.
D. Rajasthan (Nagaur)	Bhangi	Sweeping and scavenging	Taken up agriculture along with traditional occupation.
E. Maharashtra (Jalgaon)	Chamar	Leather work	Left the traditional work of leather.
F. Rajasthan (Udaipur) (Bharatpur)	Jatava	Leather work	Left handling of carcass of cattle since last 4/5 years.
G. Maharashtra (Nasik)	Mahar	Village watchmen menials and cultivators	Left handling of carcass of cattle.
H. Maharashtra (Wardha)	Mangs	Basket, rope and mat making	Partially handling carcass of cattle.
I. Madras (Ramanathapuram)	Parayan	Agricultural labourers	Tend to leave the traditional occupation.
J. Rajasthan (Chittorgarh)	Regar	Leather work	There is a tendency to leave leather work in favour of cultivation.
K. Punjab (Sangrur)	Sansi	Ex-criminal Tribe, hunting, theft etc.	Taken up agriculture and mending shoes.
L. Punjab (Ludhiana)	Valmiki	Sweeping	Tend to leave the traditional occupation.

5. *Op. cit.* p. 11. Adoption of higher education as a means of social uplift has also been reported in respect of 7 Scheduled Castes,

    1. Bawaria (Punjab, Ferozpur)
    2. Bhambi (Rajasthan, Nagaur)
    3. Chamar (Rajasthan, Sawai Madhopur)
    4. Musahar (Bihar, Purnea)
    5. Parayan (Madras, Ramanathapuram)
    6. Sansi (Punjab, Sangrur)
    7. Yadav (Rajasthan, Chittorgarh)

6. See R.K. Merton. Social Theory and Structure (Glencoe), The Free Press, (1962) Chapters VIII & IX, pp. 225-386.

CHAPTER SIX

Economic Conditions

IN ORDER to find out whether the economic conditions of the respondents have undergone any change over the past years, we have studied their income in three generations. Below are given the tables showing the income of the respondents, their fathers and their grandfathers.

TABLE 46

Showing monthly income of respondents

Sl. No.	Respondents	Percentage	Income
1.	205	51.25%	Between Rs. 55 and Rs. 90
2.	283	45.75%	,, 91 ,, 150
3.	4	1%	,, 151 ,, 200
4.	4	1%	,, 201 ,, 300
5.	4	1%	,, 301 ,, 650 and above

From the table it can be inferred that 205 respondents (51.25 per cent) are earning between Rs. 55 and Rs. 91 per month, 183 respondents (45.75 per cent) are drawing between Rs. 91 and Rs. 150 per month and 12 respondents (3 per cent) are getting ranging in between respectively Rs. 151 and Rs. 200, Rs. 201 and Rs. 300 and Rs. 301 and above. Thus, we find that the monthly income of the respondents ranges between Rs. 55 and Rs. 650, but the largest majority is of those earning between Rs. 55 and Rs. 90. Next largest is the number of those earning between Rs. 91 and Rs. 150. The number and percentage of those earning above Rs. 150 is very small. This means that by and large the monthly income of the respondents is one of the lowest. Occupation-wise income of the respondents is shown in the Table 47.

In the Table 47 we find that 4 (1.00 per cent) Khatik respondents doing business in bullocks are earning much more than any caste respondent under study; their earnings per month range between Rs. 350 to 600, again 14 Khatik respondents (3.5 per cent) are also getting Rs. 210 to 250 which is more than others by vegetable and fruit selling. 4 Chamar masons (1.00 per cent) stand in the third place earning Rs. 200 per month, 21 Chamar respondents and 1 Dom respondent are earning Rs. 150 by rickshaw pulling and again 26 Chamar respondents, 2 Baheliya and Bansphor respondents being in government service are also getting Rs. 150 per month, 8 Baheliya, 4 Chamar and Pasi respondents forming 20 respondents are drawing Rs. 125 by cultivation, 1 Pasi respondent driving tonga to earning Rs. 120, 5 Dhobi respondents on account of starting laundry are getting Rs. 115, 1 Pasi respondent is drawing Rs. 110 to 130 by carpentary, 40 Kanjar respondents are earning Rs. 150 per month by dressing flour chakkies and stone cutting, 12 Khatik, 9 Pasi and 39 Bansphors are getting Rs. 100 per month by pig husbandry and basket making, 1 Dom respondent working in a clinic is getting Rs. 95 per month, 1 Chamar car driver and 36 Chamar shoe-makers are drawing Rs. 90 per month, 36 Musahar respondents are getting Rs. 85 per month through dona and pattal making, 16 Chamar agricultural labourers, 10 Pasi respondents (Agricultural labourers) in all, 26 in number are drawing Rs. 75 per month, 18 Dom respondents are also getting Rs. 75 per month, 1 Pasi munimgir and 19 Nat respondents (beggars and acrobats) are getting Rs. 70 per month, 8 Chamar tanners are getting Rs. 65 per month, 25 Dhobi are getting Rs. 60 by washing of clothes as well as 25 cobblers also belong to this category (Chamar respondents), 1 Nat respondent is getting Rs. 55 to Rs. 60 by palladari and 4 Musahars (1 water carrier and 3 market labourers) are, also, earning Rs. 55 to Rs. 60 per month.

When the respondents were asked to indicate their savings, 4 Khatik respondents (1 per cent) said that they saved money ranging

TABLE 47

Showing occupation and income of the respondents

Sl. No.	*Type of occupation*	*No. doing*	*Per-centage*	*Caste*	*No.*	*Average monthly income*
1.	Business in Bullocks	4	1%	Khatik	4	Rs. 150 to 600
2.	Fruit & Vegetable selling	14	3.5%	Khatik	14	„ 210 to 250
3.	Masonry	4	1%	Chamar	4	„ 200
4.	Rickshaw pulling	22	5.5%	Chamar	21	„ 150
				Dom	1	
5.	Govt. service	29	7.25%	Chamar	26	„ 150
				Baheliya	2	
				Bansphor	1	
6.	Agriculture	20	5%	Baheliya	8	„ 125
				Chamar	4	
				Pasi	8	
7.	Tonga Driving	1	0.25%	Pasi	1	„ 120
8.	Laundry	5	1.25%	Dhobi	5	„ 115
9.	Carpentary	1	0.25%	Pasi	1	„ 110 to 130
10.	Stone cutting and Dressing of Flour chakkies	40	10%	Kanjar	40	„ 105
11.	Piggery & Basket making	60	15%	Khatik	12	„ 100
				Pasi	9	
				Bansphor	39	
12.	Clinic job	1	0.25%	Dom	1	„ 95
13.	Car driving (1) Shoe making (35)	36	9%	Chamar	36	„ 90
14.	Dona & Pattal making	36	9%	Musahar	36	„ 85
15.	Ariculture labour and scavenging	44	11.0%	Chamar	16	„ 75
				Pasi	10	„
				Dom	18	„
16.	Muneemgiri, Piggery and Acrobatics	20	5%	Pasi	1	„ 70
				Nat	19	
17.	Tannery	8	2%	Chamar	8	„ 65
18.	Washing of clothes & Cobblery	25	6.25%	Dhobi	25	„ 60
		25	6 25%	Chamar	25	„ 60
19.	Palladari	1	0.25%	Nat	1	„ 55
20.	Water carrying and Market labour	4	1%	Musahar	4	„ 55

between Rs. 150 to Rs. 161 per month, and the 14 Khatik respondents (3.5 percent) reported to have saved Rs. 70 per month while 4 Chamar masons Rs. 45 and 22 rickshaw pullers saved only Rs. 15 per month, the remaining persons disclosed that their saving was nil. Savings of respondents are indicated in the Table 48 as under.

TABLE 48

Showing distribution and savings among the respondents

Sl. No.	*Respondents*	*Percentage*	*Caste*	*Savings in Rupees*
1.	4	1%	Khatik	Between Rs. 150 to Rs. 161
2.	14	3.5%	Khatik	Rs. 70
3.	4	1%	Chamars (Masons)	Rs. 45
4.	22	5.5%	21 Chamar 1 Dom	Rs. 15
5.	356	89%	Remaining all castes	Nil

From the tables above, we deduce that the Khatik respondents on account of business in bullocks and selling of vegetables and fruits earn more and as a result of which their savings are significant, 4 Chamar masons have also shown their propensity to save, again 21 Chamar respondents and 1 Dom respondent driving rikshaw have also a saving tendency and the remaining respondents on account of their meagre income do not show any saving at all. This leads us to the conclusion that the Khatik respondents save for investment in business and capital formation while the rickshaw pullers save because rickshaws require repair and replacement of parts.

Income of Fathers

Table 49 shows the income of respondent's fathers :

With regard to the income of the fathers of respondents, we have four income groups as indicated in the Table 49. In the first group comes only 1 respondent whose monthly income is

TABLE 49

Showing distribution of income of respondents' fathers

Sl. No.	*Respondents fathers*	*Percentage*	*Income*
1.	1	0.25%	Rs. 45
2.	64	16%	Rs. 25 to Rs. 30
3.	215	53.75%	Rs. 18 to Rs. 22
4.	120	30%	Rs. 15 to Rs. 20

Rs. 45; in the second, third and fourth group are those who earn Rs. 25 to Rs. 30, Rs. 18 to Rs. 22 and Rs. 15 to Rs. 20 respectively.

Grandfathers' Generation and Income

Grandfather's income is given below in the Table 50.

TABLE 50

Showing distribution of grandfathers' income

Sl. No.	*Grandfathers*	*Percentage*	*Income*
1.	140	35%	Between Rs. 10 to Rs. 15
2.	260	65%	Between Rs. 16 to Rs. 20

In the grandfather's generation we have only two income groups. In the first group we have 140 grandfathers (35 per cent) while in the second group 260 grandfathers (65 per cent) are included. Both the groups show quite meagre income. It can easily be inferred here that in the past every family was supposed to be joint family and as such it was not possible to maintain a large family even at the subsistence level with such a meagre income. As a result, the grandfathers' generation had to go under heavy indebtedness.

If a comparative study is made of the three generations of the respondents, it will be found that the respondents' generation looks quite better regarding income and saving. Although such comparison is not appropriate because the value of the rupee has also declined over the years. In the fathers' and grandfathers' generation, more commodities could be commanded with a little money while in the respondents' generation, despite more earnings, one cannot buy more things. However, from their style of living, food and drink, house and health, it looks that the respondents are better off than before.

Standard of living

Standard of living represents the natural or physical conditions of a certain minima of existence.[1] The people under study consume mostly kodo, barley, cheap millets and maize. They largely depend on local produce, such as, maize, pulses, peas (*mutter*). Maize and *muttar* are consumed as *chabena* in the breakfast with onions. Their flour is also used for making breads and is eaten with the salt and onion. Barley is also used as 'sattu' (grind barley) during the summer season. Vegetables are taken rarely and often as a substitute for dal (curry). During winter season, they take sags (raw leaves of muttar, bathuva, sarson etc.) from the fields. The Chamars and Doms eat carrion. The Khatiks keep mahuva for consumption during the rainy season. The Pasis, Dom (Hindu) and Khatiks kill two pigs a year for home consumption. The diet of Khatiks, constitutes dal, fish and meat. The Dhobis take both rice and wheat and supplement it occasionally with curd, mustard oil and gur.

The Doms even today eat the leavings of almost every one. They have vegetables, pulses, rice and onion or pickles. The Dhobis and Baheliyas have, however, better standard of food. Next to them come Pasis, Chamars, Khatiks and others. Tobacco is the most important conventional necessity of the scheduled castes. Consumption of 'tari' (toddy) does not appear to have declined. The Doms take 'tari' almost every day in the evening. Pasis take tari more often than Chamars. Almost every Dhobi, Khatik, Dom and Kanjar spends 50 paise to a rupee per month on betel and tobacco.

Dhobis and Baheliyas are better clad and have adopted the garments of high castes. The Pasis and Khatiks come second, and the remaining castes follow them. Most of the people go barefooted during summer using an umbrella. It is also very significant point to note here that metalwares have completely replaced the earthen vessels in kitchens of the Scheduled Castes. Even the poorest amongst them have a jug, a tumbler and a kettle. The Dhobis, Baheliyas and Pasis have better and more untensils than others. The ornaments used by these people are generally made of silver. However, the Dhobi and Baheliya ladies have golden earlets. The greater proportion of the scheduled caste families possess only one cot or at the most two to three cots. During winter, the Chamars, Kanjars, Nats, Musahars and Bansphors sleep on the ground and use paddy straw as bedding. They use quilts which is simply a thick mattress of rags. Even in summer days they sleep on the ground on account of paucity of sufficient number of cots. The Dhobis, Baheliyas, Pasis and Khatiks possess adequate cots.

To conclude, their diet hardly provides the essential of nutrition in proper proportion. Anaemia is not uncommon amongst them, the weak and frail body coupled with minor or major ailment affects the economic position of the individual and the group. Frequent use of distilled liquor has also deprived the Doms, Chamars, Musahars, Nats, Dhobis and Bansphors, Kanjars as well of their savings, on the one hand and has, also, seriously impaired their health on the other.

Magnitude of Indebtedness

In order to assess the magnitude of indebtedness in the country, a general survey was carried out in the year 1954 under government auspices, but its observations and recommendations did not relate specifically to the scheduled castes. It was only in the year 1961 that the Registrar General of India published the extent of indebtedness among the scheduled castes which is given in the Table 51 in both rural and urban areas, statewise :

Extent of Indebtedness

In the Table 51 distribution of debt born in rural and urban areas of the State of Uttar Pradesh shows that 62.55 per cent of the scheduled caste families are running under debt in the villages while in the urban areas the percentage is however, 50.27 per cent which is slight lower than the former.

However, the size of indebtedness among the scheduled castes under study does not seem to be alarming nor enormous as it used to be 30 years back. Details of indebtedness in two generations are given in the Table 52 caste-wise :

TABLE 51

Showing distribution of indebtedness of scheduled castes in different states

Sl. No.	Name of State	Percentage of the scheduled caste families under debt	
		Rural	Urban
1.	Andhra Pradesh	69.66%	49.41%
2.	Assam	47.51%	20.40%
3.	Bihar	65.99%	54.49%
4.	Gujarat	45.24%	54.64%
5.	Jammu and Kashmir	52.69%	16.45%
6.	Kerala	60.61%	46.82%
7.	Madhya Pradesh	65.46%	41.06%
8.	Tamil Nadu	65.33%	57.75%
9.	Maharashtra	48.69%	44.78%
10.	Mysore	65.52%	61.22%
11.	Orissa	49.38%	24.07%
12.	Punjab	63.84%	44.20%
13.	Rajasthan	61.14%	63.79%
14.	Uttar Pradesh	62.55%	50.27%
15.	West Bengal	55 25%	22.83%
16.	Central Areas	78.56%	65.06%

TABLE 52

Showing extent of indebtedness per family

Sl. No.	Name of Caste	Fathers' generation debt in Rs.	Respondent's generation debt in Rs.
1.	Dom	450 to 700	200 to 300
2.	Chamar	650 to 900	300 to 375
3.	Kanjar	200 to 300	170
4.	Musahar	400 to 450	200 to 250
5.	Bansphor	300 to 500	120 to 250
6.	Nat	450 to 600	100 to 150
7.	Dhobi	300 to 500	200 to 300
8.	Khatik	350 to 400	Nil
9.	Pasi	150 to 200	Nil
10.	Baheliya	Nil	Nil

The Table shows that Chamar respondents' fathers were largely affected by the toll of indebtedness. Doms were second, Nats were third, Bansphors were fourth, Musahars were fifth, Dhobis were sixth, Khatik were seventh, Kanjars' fathers were eighth and Pasis' fathers were ninth while Baheliya respondents' parents were free from it. In the respondents' generation the order seems to have changed largely. The Khatik, Pasi and Baheliya respondents indicate that they are no longer under debt whereas Chamar, Doms, Dhobis, Musahars, Bansphors, Nats and Kanjars say that though they are indebted, the enormity of debt is not, alarming, even so they are still under its burden. In order to know the causes of indebtedness, the respondents were asked the question : "Why are you running under debt ?" 330 respondents (82.5 per cent) replied that they had to spend a good deal on drinks and social ceremonies besides the basic necessities of life. Their ceremonial occasions were always accompanied by music and drinks. This conspicuous consumption was a big charge on their income and, therefore, they were forced to borrow money. Further they reported that if they do not comply with the expectations of their community, the caste panchayats impose heavy fines and inflict corporal punishment on them. They, therefore, have to spend lavishly on festivities.

Addiction to liquor has seriously affected the Dom, Chamar, Dhobi, Musahar, Bansphor, Kanjar and Nat respondents and simultaneously has also impaired their health. To the next question whether they are aware of the harmful effects of the liquor, 330 respondents replied that they had no alternative but to drink for merrymaking. While 70 respondents (17.5 per cent) said they had no money, for extravagance, but they take drinks on very special occasions, such as, marriage of their sons. It is very difficult to gauge the psychological burden of the indebtedness, but there is hardly any doubt about the fact that it destroys family happiness and individual peace of mind while those under its burden find themselves sinking into a state of weariness and hopeless apathy.

The 330 respondents (82.5 per cent) further reported the indebtedness had become a normal or almost an inescapable aspect of their existence. The custom of marriage, death and hospitality pressurizes them to take credit and they must observe them because these occasions provide them with escape from the dull routine of their life. On the economic side, they have to depend upon the local grocer (Bania) or Sahukar who supplies them consumption goods on credit. Our study, therefore, provides the following causes for the indebtedness of the scheduled castes under study :

1. they have small sources of their income.
2. they addict to liquors as a necessity and, thus, major part of their income is squandered away on drinks.
3. they are forced to celebrate their festivities with pomp and show by their own community failing which they are fined by their caste panchayats. For fear of ex-communication and heavy fines, they comply with the expectations of their community and caste panchayat.
4. large scale celebrations and festivities like marriage and death entail large expenditure.[2]

When the respondents, were asked to indicate the sources of borrowing money, the respondents gave the following sources shown in the Table 53 below :

TABLE 53

Showing sources of borrowing money

Sl. No.	*Sources of borrowing money*	*Respondents*	*Percentage*
1.	Professional money lenders	306	76.5%
2.	Agriculturist money lenders	8	2%
3.	Government agencies	10	2.5%
4.	From relatives	10	2.5%
5.	No source	66	16.5%

In answer to the next question "Why do they borrow money from the grocer and not the co-operative credit society?" 314 respondents replied that the money lender readily offered unsecured loans. There were no formalities, no documents and no cumbersome procedures. Second, the grocer recognised their earnings and some land or property as good security while the governmental agencies had an elaborate procedure. Third, the money lender did not make any delay in the disbursement of loans. When the debtor approached him, he made the cash available. Fourth, the money lender was generally near at hand in the village or city. He knew the debtor personally and his family background and the circumstances leading to the debtor's need of money. Fifth, the government advanced loans for productive purposes and not to meet social obligations whereas the money lender extended the loans for both purposes. The money lender also floated loans for funerals, marriages, maintenance and clothing. Sixth, the money lender had no objection in accepting cash or kind[3] while the repayment of loan was being made.

In answer to the question whether the money lenders resorted to some unscrupulous means of recovery of dues, 21 respondents (5.25 per cent) said that they paid towards redemption of their debt but to their utmost surprise that their regular payment was counted against interest and the capital borrowed, thus, always remained unpaid. The transactions between the Scheduled Castes and the money lenders are generally oral. While 20 Nat respondents (5 per cent) reported that the position of the money lender or Sahukar was impregnable on account of the absence of an alternative source of credit. Although they had an alternative credit system in their locality, yet it did not function properly. They related to further that they joined a co-operative society in the neighbouring village and deposited their share in it. Later it was discovered that the total assets of the society were robbed away and the society was declared a defunct body by its president. Under such circumstances, how can the requirements of the people be met by co-operation.[4]

Hunger for Land

The scheduled castes are also land hungry like the scheduled tribes. There are several reasons for it besides the common desire to possess land. One is that the scheduled castes are growing in numbers and the land which they possess is shortening alarmingly. The scheduled castes under study have holdings ranging between (1 Bigha to 11 Bighas) of land. By and large their land is of poor quality. Under these circumstances, it is not surprising that there should be an ever increasing hunger for more and better land. The Table 54 shows the size of holdings per family :

TABLE 54

Showing distribution of agricultural land per family

Sl. No.	*Size of holdings*		
	1—4 bighas	*5—8 bighas*	*9—14 bighas*
1.	4 Chamars 1%	8 Pasis 2%	8 Baheliyas 2%

From the Table we infer that we have three categories of tenants :

1. Those with holdings from 1 to 4 bighas of land
2. Those with holdings from 5 to 8 bighas of land
3. Those with holdings from 9 to 14 bighas of land.[5]

Poor soil, small holdings, poor technique of cultivation and the burden of indebtedness have been largely responsible for the many handicaps which the scheduled castes have suffered for years. Even after independence, the odds continue against them, though sufficient remedial measures have been taken by the government.[6]

Cottage Industry

The existing low potential of agriculture coupled with the present low level of supplementary employment is in no small measure, the cause of the destitution of the scheduled castes. Those who have neither land nor any substantial occupation are the worst affected. The last 33 years have, no doubt, brought a spectacular change in the conditions of the people but the developmental schemes have not affected every class equally. The lot of the scheduled castes still leaves much to be desired. When the respondents were asked, 'Why do you not start poultry farm or piggery ?' Cent percent respondents from among the Chamar, Baheliya and Khatik castes replied that they would prefer to die than to contaminate their religion by adopting these trades. Here, there is a big social obstacle in the way of their development. They would not take to trades which they consider socially degrading whatever be the economic benefits, they promise.

The quantum of average employment available to a casual adult male agricultural labour is about 153 days in the area.[7] This points to the definite conclusion that we cannot look to land alone for a satisfactory solution of the unemployment problem.

The respondents under study stated with surprise that there was not much contact between them and those incharge of scheduled caste problems at the governmental level. Efforts at spreading the village industries have been most superficial. The Chamars of the district have forsaken the traditional occupation of lifting the dead cattle which has resulted in further economic strain on them.

The problem of the destitution of the scheduled castes under study can be tackled through the development of the village and cottage industries. Development of industries both cottage and village conceives a plan to combat poverty by providing opportunity for work and developing the local resources through improved techniques in the field of production. It is a mass approach to the problems of underemployment, and unemployment. The Patel Commission has also recommended that more emphasis should be laid on the expansion of industries in Deoria, Azamgarh, Ghazipur and Jaunpur districts. The area under study has good prospects for the development of certain small scale industries notably amongst them being the consumer goods industries and the processing industries. Palash leaves used as dining platters is one such small scale industry which can be developed successfully and the Musahars who are engaged in this trade can earn more if it is started on a co-operative basis. There is a wide market for the platters. It does not involve any technical or transport problem either they can be locally dumped into the market. Besides poultry, farming and fishery can also be introduced even though some of the respondents consider them filthy undertakings.

There is some scope for expansion of cottage industries; such as, bee-keeping, rope-making, soap-making, net-making for fishing, basket making also. The scheduled castes can be gainfully employed in these industries. Manufacture of bidis has also a good scope for expansion. Processing of maize can, also, be carried out since we have adequate sources of supply of maize in the district. Tannery can also be introduced, but it carries a social stigma among the Chamars today. To create an urge among the scheduled castes for going in trades, we require the incentive of the local leaders besides that of the government. Hand pounding of rice in Machhli Shahar and Shahaganj and broom-making in Kerakat sub-division can also be promising trades. Thus, the district has rich basic resources and the backing of a vast agricultural community. It is, therefore, now a question of effort, organisation and practical schemes. The Government provides grants-in-aid upto Rs. 500 to an individual and Rs. 5,000 to a co-operative society for starting a new industry. This aid is only extended to those young educated men and women who have sufficient knowledge of the particular trade they want to start, but cannot execute it because of their small sources. For obtaining such aid the applications have to be submitted to the district Harijan Officer and Social Welfare Officer in the district. This facility may be extended to other people also.

The Problem of Public Health

Quite a lot of good work has been done in the field of public health, especially malaria control in the post independent era. But there is a vast bee-way to be made up and medical facilities in the rural areas are still far from adequate. The normal health of the scheduled castes under study cannot be said to be good. A poor health is always an economic burden.

The scheduled castes covered in this enquiry suffer from many diseases. In some villages where water is dirty, they become easily susceptible to intestinal and skin diseases. Diarrhoea, dysentry, cholera and small pox are also not infrequent. The respondents appreciated the role of anti-malaria agencies which had several times visited their houses. Equally they praised the Family Planning units which often contacted them for the propagation of contraceptives. We have the greatest paucity of medical personnel and qualified nurses because we have failed to create the necessary urge in the men and women of the medical profession to offer themselves for service in rural areas.

Some public health centres are functioning in the district. The scheduled castes go there and get medicine. The respondents did not cite any case of discriminatory treatment meted out to them by the doctors.

Water Supply

All the castes under study except Nats, Bansphors, Musahars have their separate wells in their localities. The Nats, do not have any water pot in their village. They have to fetch water everyday from a distance of four miles. The Kanjars of Kheradin (Marihau) living in colony have pucca well which has no shed. The Musahars and the Bansphors living in Dhanipur have neither water taps nor any well. They experience great difficulties in water supply.

The Problem of Housing

The housing problem, of the scheduled castes can be viewed from four aspects, shelter, sanitation, cultural taste and comparative cost.

Generally, the Scheduled Castes are living on the outskirts of the villages under thatched houses. They are placed in unhealthy surroundings where the filth of the village is thrown. Due to social circumstances, they are content to live in miserable, dirty and insanitary houses without proper doors and either far, too, open to the weather or completely lacking in ventilations. Where colonies for Scheduled Castes have been constructed, the Scheduled Caste families have developed a real pride in having a good house. The Chamars of Khetasarai proper, the Kanjars of Kheradinganj and Doms living in the city have been living in colonies and they look quite happy in their small houses. Other castes like Khatiks, Dhobis and the Baheliyas on account of their better economic conditions have an attractive lay out of their houses. Our observations lead was to the conclusion that those who have government quarters have their houses more neat and tidy. The abominable small is only associated with those Chamar houses where tannery is done (tanning is becoming now uncommon). A typical dwelling of a Scheduled Caste family consists of a two roomed cottage with mud walls and a thatch. But the houses of Dhobis, Baheliyas, a few Chamars and Khatiks, Kanjars (40), Pasis and Doms are made of bricks and their roofs of tiles. Almost all the cases under study have their own houses. All the houses have roughly one door.

The Nat's houses, of course, have a rough wooden frame with wattle and slab panelling swinging on two vertical wooden pivots. Usually the rooms in the house of Dhobis, Baheliyas and Pasis are 10 feet long and 6 feet wide. A serious defect in a normal scheduled caste dwelling is lack of proper ventilation. The respondents when asked about having no ventilation replied that houses without ventilation prevented the mosquitos and other stinging insects from coming in and in different seasons these houses were kept ready with the change of weather.

The scheduled castes living in the suburbs of the city have also their own houses. The Doms have their quarters under colony scheme which with water taps are more neat and tidy than those their counterparts the Bansphors and Musahars. The Bansphors and Musahars have no arrangement for latrine, any lighting while the Doms possess common latrines. The houses of Bansphors and Musahars are without doors and entirely made of straw and bamboo and open to all weathers. It may also, be mentioned here with regard to the housing scheme started by the Government that the scheduled castes have now begun to expect government to do everything for them and, thus, their self-reliance is diminishing. Instead, pauperism is developing amongst them. The most important point, therefore, here is that the housing scheme should only benefit those who are in real need of houses.

All too, often, the benefits of this programme have gone to the well-to-do scheduled castes elsewhere some of whom may already have a house. At the same time the really poor Nats, Musahar and the Bansphors have not benefited for they could not pay their own contribution in cash. Grant-in-aid under the housing scheme for the construction of a house is sanctioned by the government upto Rs. 900 (the estimated cost of a house is generally considered to be Rs. 1200) and the rest Rs. 300 are borne by the grantee. Recently provisions have, also, been made by the government for the purchase of land for the construction of a house. For the purchase of a plot, a sum of Rs. 750 is advanced as grant-in-

TABLE 55

Showing amount of grant-in-aid sanctioned for the construction of well and hand pump by the government of U.P.

Sl. No.	*Items*	*Amount of grant-in-aid given*	*Percentage of the expenditure*
1.	For construction of well	Rs. 1,000	75% of the total expenditure
2.	Hand pump	From 75 to Rs. 225	25% expenditure to be borne by the grantee.

aid. In 1969-70 the Uttar Pradesh state sanctioned Rs. 50,000 for this purpose. The government also floats grant-in-aid on the following items in the Table 55.

In 1967-68 the government of Uttar Pradesh allocated Rs. 5,00,000 for the construction of wells and hand pipes, in 1968-69 Rs. 10,00,000 and in the year 1969-70 only Rs. 2,00,000. It will not be out of way to emphasise here that the government should not follow hurried programme for the construction of houses for the scheduled castes with a view to fulfil the targets. During the field work it was found that the houses made under the colony scheme have a weak structure and the people living in them feel insecure. Second, no legislative measures have been adopted by any State government for providing facilities for scheduled castes. The State of Bihar, Maharashtra, Orissa, Uttar Pradesh, Mysore, Gujarat, Kerala and Madhya Pradesh have, however, taken some executive measures for this purpose. The Government of Uttar Pradesh have drawn up a tentative scheme for the construction of over 2,000 quarters for scheduled caste employees by granting subsidies to the municipal boards. Figures available from 25 out of 52 districts of the State show that about 43 per cent of the scheduled castes are owners of permanent structures though they have no proprietary rights on the land on which these structures are built.[8]

NOTES AND REFERENCES

1. Classical economists believed that standard of living meant the cost of labour as a factor of production and the Austrian School emphasized its importance in connection with the theory of consumption. Marshall conceived of it as the activities adjusted to wants or as the standard of comfort.

2. The special Assistant Agent, Bhadrachalam gave the following causes for indebtedness among the scheduled castes and scheduled tribes : meagre income due to infertile land, ignorance of equitable price system, adherence to panchayat (caste panchayats) decisions and payment of fines imposed by them and social celebrations at large scale, quoted in Report of The Scheduled Areas and Scheduled Tribes Commission Vol. I, 1960-61, p. 200.

   (ii) See also the Report of the Commissioner for Scheduled Castes and Scheduled Tribes for the year 1959-60 p. 71.

3. The all India Rural Credit Survey also reveals that there is normally a timelag of at least three months if not more between the date of application

and date of disbursement of loans by government departments. But in the case of the money lender, there is no delay in disbursing the loan-amount. (The report was published in the year 1954).

4. Report of the Committee of Co-operative Credit (S.N. 18 p. 203) has recommended a dynamic programme of agricultural plans. The primary society should not deny a loan to a person on the ground that he does not own land.

5. The land per capita in the country is less than an acre as against 7.5 acre in the U.S.A. and 4.5 acres in the U.S.S.R. On an average a person dependant on agriculture in India has 1.6 acres of land. There are wide variations from region to region as the Report of the Working Group on Co-operative Farming, Vol. I (Ministry of Community Development and Co-operatives) p. 8 calculates as under :

1. North region	—1.01 acres
2. Eastern region	—1.25 ,,
3. Southern region	—1.17 ,,
4. Western region	—2.29 ,,
5. North Western region	—2.56 ,,
6. Central region	—2.56 ,,

Note : 1 bigha of land is equal to 65 decimals.

6. The U.P. Zamindari Abolition and the Land Reform Act, 1950 safeguard the rights of all tenure holders, bhumidars and sirdars, including unscheduled castes irrespective of caste and creed. Under the same act preference is given to the landless labourers for allotment of agricultural lands. In the State of Uttar Pradesh 10,684 acres of land has been so far, given to the scheduled castes. Most of this land was obtained and given to them through the good offices of the Bhoodan Yajna Samity.

Note : Usha Rao in her study. 'Deprived Castes in India' (1981) records 2/3 of the total cultivating households among scheduled castes in 1961 had land, less than 5 acres (p. 341).

7. Report on Agricultural Labour in India, Vol. I published by Ministry of Labour and Employment, Govt. of India (p. 72) calculates 197 days in the plains.

8. L. M. Srikant : Report of the Commissioner for Scheduled Castes and Scheduled Tribes for 1953, p. 84.

CHAPTER SEVEN

Education

OUR COUNTRY is growing more and more education conscious and this consciousness is also reflected among the backward sections of the country. Literacy among the scheduled castes on the whole is still very low. The general percentage of literacy in India for males was 24.88 per cent, for females it was 7.87 per cent and for everybody it was 16.61 per cent.[1] In recent decades, this percentage has gone to more than 25 per cent for everybody. The scheduled caste percentage has been estimated at about 6.5 per cent all over India. In the State of Uttar Pradesh 20.9 per cent of the total population of the scheduled caste is now engaged in higher education while in Rajasthan and Bihar the percentage is respectively 16.7 per cent and 14.1 per cent.[2] The programme Evaluation Organisation which conducted a study of the problems of extension of primary education in rural areas found that the enrolment of Harijan[3] children had increased more than two and a half times in 1961 as compared to 1951. The roll of Harijan children showed an increase from 13.6 per cent in 1951 to 16.1 per cent in 1961 (only primary education). In the secondary and higher stages, the enrolment is low in all the states. In the states of Uttar Pradesh, Rajasthan and Bihar, the enrolment of scheduled castes for higher education is 4.3 per cent, 1.5 per cent and 3.4 per cent respectively. The urge for education among the scheduled castes under study is also quite encouraging. Regarding the educational attainments of the 400 respondents, 318 respondents (79.50 per cent) are illiterate : 9 respondents (2.25 per cent) are educated upto 1st standared, 12 respondents (3 per cent) are educated upto 2nd standard, 16 respondents (4 per cent) upto 3rd standard, 5 respondents (1.25 per cent) are simply literate, 9 respondents (2.25 per cent) upto 4th standard, 6 respondents (1.50 per cent) upto 6th standard, 4 respondents (1 per cent) upto 7th standard, 6 respondents (1.50 per cent) have read upto 8th class, 2 respondents (0.50 per cent) upto 9th standard, 3 respondents (0.75 per cent) are middle class passed, 1 respondent is (0.25 per cent) high school passed, 1 (0.25 per cent) inter passed, 1 (0.25 per cent) is a Sahitya Ratna and 1 (0.25 per cent) is an M.A. passed.

It is strange enough to note here that the education of the wives of the respondents is nil. Out of 400 respondents, only 2 (0.50 per cent) respondents fathers and grandfathers had primary education and 398 respondents' (99.50 per cent) had no educational background. The Table 56 shows the educational attainments of the respondents under study.

The respondents referred to certain difficulties in the way of sending their children to school, during the field study. They feel that it is much inconvenient for them to send their grown-up boys or girls to the schools because they (children) constituted an economic preposition for their families and, therefore, it will entail dislocation of traditional pattern of division of labour in the families if they were sent to school. Girls lend help to their mothers in the work at home and sometimes, in the fields also particularly in the sowing, and reaping seasons. Many parents cannot afford to send their children to school on account of poor economic resources. In fact, free provision for book aid and scholarship by the State and the centre has surely attracted the boys and girls in bulk towards educational institutions.

Since independence, the scheduled caste boys' and girls' enrolment in the schools of the district has adequately increased. The present enrolment upto March 1970 was as below :

(i) Boys : 37078

(ii) Girls : 8902

Serious complaints came to our notice during the study as regards payment of scholarship at every stage. The respondents complained that their wards never received the scholarship on time. Various methods have been tried to obviate the delays, but none

TABLE 56

Showing educational attainments of respondents

Educational standard	*Grand fathers*		*Fathers*		*Self*		*Wife*	
	No.	*%age*	*No.*	*%age*	*No.*	*%age*	*No.*	*%age*
I	Nil	Nil	Nil	Nil	9	2.25	Nil	Nil
II	,,	,,	,,	,,	12	3.00	,,	,,
III	,,	,,	,,	,,	16	4	,,	,,
Simply literate	,,	,,	,,	,,	5	1.25	,,	,,
IV	,,	,,	2	0.50	9	2.25	,,	,,
V	,,	,,	Nil	Nil	6	1.50	,,	,,
VI	,,	,,	,,	,,	6	1.50	,,	,,
VII	,,	,,	,,	,,	4	1	,,	,,
Middle class Passed	,,	,,	,,	,,	6	1.50	,,	,,
VIII class passed	,,	,,	,,	,,	1	0.25	,,	,,
IX	,,	,,	,,	,,	3	0.75	,,	,,
High School passed	,,	,,	,,	,,	2	0.50	,,	,,
Intermediate passed	,,	,,	,,	,,	1	0.25	,,	,,
Sahitya Ratna	,,	,,	,,	,,	1	0.25	,,	,,
M.A. passed	,,	,,	,,	,,	1	0.25	,,	,,
Illiterate	,,	,,	398	99.50	318	79.50	,,	,,

has, so far, succeeded. Because of inordinate delays in the disbursement of scholarships, the scheduled caste students are compelled to borrow money for their sustenance at exorbitant rates of interest from the local money lenders and as the amount of scholarships is limited after defraying the interest charges, they have very little left for their studies.

G. W. Briggs' observation that the schools maintained at public cost are practically closed to much impure castes such the Chamars and Mahars and that both teachers and pupils in the school make it most difficult for low caste boys to sit in the classrooms,[4] is not true now. The respondents under study did not mention any such ill-treatment. Some parents, of course, murmured against the little amount of scholarship being given to their children. They asked for a greater allocation on this item.

The ideal of all education should be the transformation of men. It should not be simply equated with the amount of information that it imparts, but must be treated as a training for development of the art of habit formation. The entire conception of education should be oriented towards the improvement of the basic life conditions and the reduction of the artificial water-tight-compartments into which the society has become divided.

Education after independence has become open to all, it is no longer a monopoly of the richer classes. Therefore, the wholesale eradication of illiteracy among the scheduled castes is not an impossibility. Near about 2800 young men belonging to the scheduled castes are emerging each year with Bachelor's degrees at various educational levels.[5] Large numbers of educated young men are moving into government jobs, most of them in the lower clerical grades. Thus, in the near future, education may have a big impact on their thinking and action. The Harijan Welfare department is running the following schools in the district where the Harijans have separate facilities of schooling, lodging and boarding :

1. Primary School; Faridabad, Sujanganj (Machhli Sahar, Sub-division).
2. Primary School; Mithora (Machhli Sahar, Sub-division).
3. Primary Girls' School; Sighwaran.
4. The Harijan Boarding House; Line Bazar, Jaunpur.
5. Boarding House; Mohalla, Khasanpur, Jaunpur.
6. Library; Khetasarai, Jaunpur.
7. Pustakalaya; Beriwari, Jaunpur.
8. Primary Pathashala; Sawarhad.

'itical Participation

't changes especially the extension of adult franchise and the abolition of Zamindari have legitimised the leadership aspiration of all the castes.

The leadership aspirations of the traditionally subservient and disprivileged groups have given an unprecedented challenge to the traditionally dominant groups. The scope of informal leadership during the Zamindari period was quite large pervading all aspects of village life—economic, political, social and cultural. The abolition of Zamindari ended the officially sanctioned economic and the political hegemony of the traditionally dominant group. The introduction of new formal political institutions like the Gram Panchayat and Adult Panchayat Samiti and the Zila Parishad has brought about changes in myriad ways. The report of the Team for the study of Community Projects and National extension has recognised that the Panchayats should be strengthened not only for sustained development activities, but, also, for the effective functioning of democracy itself. Panchayat in some form or other with varying degrees of powers have always existed. It is believed that the system was first introduced by the king Prithu. In Manusmrti and Shanti Parva of the Mahabharata, there are many references to the existence of Gram sanghas (or rural communities). A description of these rural communities is also found in the Arthashastra of Kautilya who lived in 400 B.C. In the Ramayana of Valmiki, we read about the Janapadas which was, perhaps, a kind of federation of village republics.[6] The panchayats have, however, been given an entirely new constitution in modern independent India.

In fact, the village in India has been looked upon as the basic unit of administration since the earliest Vedic times. Gramini or the leader of the village is mentioned in the Rigveda (X. 62. ii, 1075). References to the Gram sabhas or the local village assemblies are found in the Jatakas as well. The village continued to be regarded as a corporate political unit throughout the post Vedic period. Thus in the Vishnu Purana and Manusmriti, the village is reckoned as the smallest political unit in the state fabric.[7] The Dharma Sutras and Dharma Snastras contain frequent references to 'grama' and 'praja' both of which terms seem to have denoted the village or town corporations.

The Indian rural republics continued to flourish during the rule of Hindus. Muslims and Peshwas till the advent of East India Company. They survived the wreck of dynasties and downfall of empires. The independent development of local government provided like the shell of the tortoise, a heaven of peace where the national culture could draw in for its own safety, when geographical storms burst over the land.[8] Sir Charles Trevellyn remarks : "One foreign conquerer after another has swept over India, but the village Municipalities have stuck to the soil like their own "kushagrass." The ideal of Panchayat Raj has been accepted by all and is spreading fast. A Panchayat is a group of recognised leaders (literally a council of five) who meet to pass judgment on judicial cases or problems or who convene to plan some undertaking or course of procedure in a matter requiring united action. The importance of panchayats in village life has increased in recent years due to the reconstruction programme associated with India's First Five Year Plan. It seems to be a basic assumption of the Planning Commission that the panchayats are democratic representative bodies which will forward the objective of the plan.[9]

Panchayats have an indispensable role to play in the rural areas; they have to safeguard the interests of the landless tenants in the community, to enforce tenancy legislation and to act as local agents of land-reforms. This optimistic faith seems now to be misplaced since panchayats are dominated by the land owning castes. Panchayats dominated by upper castes, cannot be considered as an impartial tribunal for an important purpose underlying the creation of the statutory panchayats was to make a more impartial tribunal available to the lower castes. When the respondents under study were asked to indicate whether the creation of panchayats proved helpful or not in doing some tangible things for them, 305 respondents (76.25 per cent) answered that they had done not or quite insignificant work in the direction of improving conditions of the villages. They, also, reported that different members coming from different factions in the village tried to pull down one another in the meetings of the village panchayats.[10] However, 95 (23.75 per cent) respondents admitted that the introduction of Panchayati Raj had made it possible both theoretically and practically for all to participate in the village polity on an equal footing. All the lower castes now could legitimately aspire for leadership positions in the rural areas. Any such aspiration in the past was illegitimate. The responses are tabulated further in the Table 57.

The establishment of the Panchayat Raj in the villages was a

TABLE 57

Showing responses regarding efficacy of panchayats

Sl. No.	Responses	Respondents	Percentage
1.	Panchayats have done little in improving village conditions	305	76.25%
2.	Panchayats have fared well in their mission	95	23.75%

part of the democratic process which was introduced in India after independence. Its other part was the introduction of adult franchise. Now to ascertain the extent of the participation of the scheduled castes in the democratic process, the following question was addressed to the respondents.

Have you been exercising your vote in the general elections held so far ? 210 respondents (52.5 per cent) replied that they had been exercising their right of voting in all the general elections while 190 (47.5 per cent) respondents said they went only to two polls, that is, in 1967 general elections and the mid term poll of 1971. The position of participation is indicated below in the Table 58.

TABLE 58

Showing participation in the general elections

Sl. No.	Responses	Respondents	Percentage
1.	Participated in all the general elections held so far	210	52.5%
2.	Participated only in 1967 general election and mid-term election in 1971	190	47.5%

The next question that we asked them was, 'whom did you vote in the general elections?'

(a) For the candidate of your own caste?
(b) For the candidate of any other scheduled caste?
(c) For a candidate not belonging to either of the two groups?

Their reply was that generally the selection of candidates in the elections was made by the parties concerned on the basis of the dominant caste of constituency. This was more true of the reserved constituencies than of the general ones. However, they said generally they voted for the party which was strong irrespective of whether its candidate belonged to their caste or not. Apart from this general condition they usually favour a candidate who can give them help either in the form of cash or promise. They also favour candidates who can provide them with liquor or other drinks.

When further asked to answer the question whether in the panchayat elections, they voted for the candidates of their own castes or of other castes? Cent per cent respondents said that the structural factors still played a decisive role. They obviously evaded the question but in three villages scheduled castes are represented in the gaon panchayats through their elected Pradhans. They said that the upper castes have now changed their attitude towards them and instead of taking their support for granted, they were going all the way to persuade them to vote for them. 372 respondents (93 per cent) reported that in the general elections particularly in those of 1967 and in the mid-term poll of 1971, leader from various parties approached them and assured them time and again that if they were elected on account of their favour they would serve them better and never forget their obligations. 28 respondents (7 per cent) however, had a different story to narrate, they said that they were threatened by unknown persons to cast their votes in favour of their men, failing which they would be heavily penalized. The responses are given as under in the Table 59.

TABLE 59

Showing pluralism in the elections

Sl. No.	*Responses*	*Respondents*	*Percentage*
1.	Different leaders persuaded them and contacted them time and again	372	93%
2.	Leaders or their agents threatened them to vote for their favourite	28	7%

When asked as to why they did not combine together and set-up their own candidate in the primary elections, 321 respondents (80.25 per cent) replied that they formed several different entities and were hardly a cohesive unit. Their division, thus, benefitted the upper castes, 79 respondents (19.75 per cent) stated that they did not have ample money to stand in the election nor courage to annoy the upper castes by challenging them in the election. If they did so they would suffer from their wrath. The responses are tabulated as under in the Table 60.

TABLE 60

Showing combined effort of scheduled castes in installing their own candidate

Sl. No.	Responses	Respondents	Percentage
1.	They cannot stand combined as they constituted several social entities. But they are ready to forge unity among themselves	321	80.25%
2.	They have neither ample money nor courage to annoy the upper castes	79	19.75%

When asked further to indicate whether the caste Hindus considered them as their legitimate rivals or otherwise, 307 respondents (76.75 per cent) replied that the caste Hindus had now started looking at them as their legitimate competitors and, thus, they tried consciously to retain their hold through politicking,[11] 93 respondents (23.25 per cent) did not indicate anything at all.

From what has been said above it may be concluded that the shape of the village polity is now undergoing a change; the upper castes who used to be the leaders of the polity and who obtained the support of the lower castes through sheer dominance and influence have revised their thinking. They seem to be fully aware of the fact that all interests in the village must be accommodated in the polity, otherwise, it will be difficult to organise and run it. They have, therefore, started approaching the lower castes also, and promising them to safeguard their interests if they are elected. Thus, we may say that the new trends in the social, economic and educational fields are prone to produce a climate conducive to the growth and development of pluralistic tendencies in the village polity.[12]

In the near future the scheduled castes may assert their numerical strength for political power. But at present they are not united partly on account of their diverse origins, cultural background and caste affiliations, and partly because of having no leadership of a high calibre and strong character which could forge unity among them and iron out their mutual differences.

The Panchayati Raj has failed in its prime objective of mobilising the people for development work, although it is true that it has succeeded in making all the sections of our society politically conscious. A study made by the Administrative Reform Commission shows that more than 80 per cent of the villagers are dissatisfied with the working of panchayats mainly because of rampant corruption.[13] Mandelbaum observes that new panchayats seem generally to be off to a shaky start. There is some tendency for them to become the battle ground of village factionalism. Factionalism has long been a frequent disrupter of joint village action.[14]

Our study also confirms the view that panchayats are in a poor shape because their financial and other powers are limited. The gram pradhans have not translated anything effectively into action. The administrative functions of the panchayats—watch and ward, control and regulation of markets, slaughter houses, sanitation and health are hardly recognised in practice. The economic functions, development of agricultural techniques, promotion of cottage industries and animal husbandry are not being properly executed. Nor are the social functions—education, recreation, maternity and child welfare being performed satisfactorily.

One way to improve matters is to make the panchayats subject to stricter official scrutiny. There is clearly a need for more stringent safeguard to make sure that panchayati raj institutions do not become instruments for the distribution of patronage in rural areas. We require enough political courage, personal honesty and will to work to discipline these wayward institutions.

Caste Panchayats

The caste panchayats are equally important side by side. The formal institutions have not, however, been able to do away with the popularity and sanctity of informal institutions notably the caste panchayats. The judicial functions of the traditional panchayats and their role in regulating moral conduct, still reflect their powerful influence. Dhillon describes these panchayats as "Hookah smoking groups of the various factions."[15] Besides, they also establish certain general standards for instance in setting limits to dowries, in the number of persons to participate in a marriage party or in the amount of money spent on wedding gifts. The moral issues involving kidnapping, illicit sex relations and cheating etc. are also decided by these panchayats. The caste panchayats operate today almost as efficaciously as they did in the past. But the jurisdiction of each panchayats is confined to its respective caste. The caste panchayats settle all disputes by avoiding recourse to endless litigation in costly law courts, the proceedings of which are totally incomprehensible to the scheduled castes.

All the scheduled castes under study have their panchayats; the caste panchayats have their panchayats 'chowdharis', the Chiefs who, sometimes, are hereditary and sometimes, unanimously recognised. These Chiefs wield all the power for the castes concerned and decide even those matters which by their nature the proper jurisdiction of civil courts. The caste panchayats exercise their jurisdiction over the caste as such and not the caste of a particular village; their jurisdiction is, of course, limited to a fixed territorial area but it extends over several villages. The caste panchayats are very strict in awarding punishments to the erring members of the caste. The Nat caste Panchayats, for instance award humiliating punishment to the guilty. His face may be blackened or one moustache or eye brow may be shaved by the caste panchayats is also awarded, but this is becoming rare now. The Dhobi caste panchayats effect compromises and arrange the partition of family property under dispute. They, also, arrange return of wives who have deserted their husbands. During the field study, it was found that in a Dhobi caste panchayat meeting, a man was heavily fined on account of a serious offence of adultry. He had to give feast to the brotherhood or face ex-communication. He was also asked by the chowdharies to spend the fine on giving sweets and drinks to the biradari (brotherhood), and if any amount was left after that, to use the same for the construction of a well or temple.

The Khatik panchayats are very influential in settling disputes, in enforcing promises of marriage and in inflicting corporal punishment on the offender. During the field work, we noticed an incident. A Khatik put his mother in a canvass bag and threw her in the river Ganges. The news after a week of the incident spread in the Biradari (caste). As a result, the meeting of the caste panchayat was summoned and chowdharies (council of the chiefs of the panchayat) rebuked him for his cowardly act and asked him to arrange a feast (Bhoj) for five hundred persons belonging to his community and to go to Varanasi for atoning his sin. Some members, present in the meeting insisted for a hundred shoe-strokes to be given to the offender.

Independent India has witnessed the waning power of these caste organisations. Our informants told us that when a Chowdhari (chief of the caste) died, his successor was not always elected or recognised, for the summoning of a panchayat proved too much for them. A member when asked 'Do you fear ex-communication if you infringed the caste rules ? He replied that he did not see any danger of ex-communication now. Moreover, man as boycotted by his caste man could enjoy privilege elsewhere.

The caste panchayats no longer discharge their duties faithfully and are, often, found showing consideration for the rich. The offenders now, do not bother about the dictates of the caste panchayats. Cases of enticement, adultry etc. are now taken to courts of law whereas in the past they were decided by the panchayats. The Chamar respondents said that the weakening of the traditional panchayats had helped in bringing about greater individual liberty and a better adjustment to changed social and economic conditions. However, the institution of caste panchayat still possesses considerable vitality and has an important place in the life of the people.

Political Affiliations

The ruling congress party commands the allegiance of the scheduled castes. There is no visible independent political awareness among them. The Socialists or Communists have not made even a little headway among them. The Socialists being perennially split up, have not won their support. The Communists have also been torn due to their various factions and hence have no roots at all among the scheduled castes. In Andhra and Kerala the communists have, no doubt, made some headway in arousing the caste sentiments in their favour. But beyond temporary, ad-hoc-adjustments, these caste adjustments have not been able to serve any positive political purpose. The educated youths among some of the castes under study have developed some fascination for the Arjak Sangh, but they have not begun in real earnest to rally round this organisation

When asked, why do they not take active part in the organisation, they replied that they were interested in employment and better living. All this is only possible by following the Congress Party. Politics has become rather a game of clever manipulation, not a pursuit really deserving of dedicated man.[16] The informants further asserted that they would follow the Congress Party till things would not become difficult for them. The day, they realize that things have become difficult, they will not be shy of changing their loyalties.

During the 1967 election and later in the mid-term poll in Jaunpur, the scheduled castes favoured Jad Sangh in one constituency while in another constituency they threw in their lot with the Congress Party. They admitted the fact that they were easily won over by a little money and promise of little position. Harold R. Issacs reports almost the same findings in his studies at all India level.[17] The respondents told us that by placing their own men in better positions they would be able to command more power and bolster their position in the economic and opportunity structures. In democratic India, they now have the opportunity to do this as citizens and voters. Thus, elections to legislative posts have assumed great significance; they are the structural and legitimate means with which to capture power, at least the power of authority in Indian society.[18]

It was also observed during the field work that an M.L.A. is honoured more than an office bearer of a party organisation. Those who occupy political offices have access to real patronage and, thus, are able to do something concrete for their constituents. The party officers, unless, they also hold some elected post have no such power and are in a far weaker position to gain support for their views. This indicates that party organisation does not have much significance in the public eye, the M.L.A. who is a symbol of the ruling party and a dispenser of party favours has greater value to the public than the organisation itself.[19]

As regards reservation quota in political sphere, an all India representation before 1967 was 477 M.L.As and 72 M.Ps in Lok Sabha. The present position after 1967 election may be summed up as in the Table 61.[19a]

Realizing the political value of the scheduled castes, the government have now increased their reservation quota in all India Central Services through UPSC Competitive tests from 12.5 per

TABLE 61

Showing an all India representation of scheduled castes in Lok Sabha and legislature

State	Lok Sabha	Legislature
Uttar Pradesh	18	89
Tamil Nadu	7	37
Bihar	7	40
Andhra Pradesh	6	43
Maharashtra	6	33
West Bengal	6	45
Madhya Pradesh	5	43
Punjab	5	33
Rajasthan	3	28
Other states	14	112

cent to 15 per cent and 16.2 per cent through recruitment. Vacancies by promotion will now be made onwards from 12.5 per cent to 15 per cent. The following tables indicate the numerical strength of scheduled castes in All India Central Services.

TABLE 62

Showing vacancies by Reservation quota

Sl. No.	Strength	Year
1.	326	On January 1, 1968
2.	371	Made in 1970

TABLE 63

Showing class IV service Reservation quota

Year 1963	Year 1968
1,86,674	1,11,115

The figures above in IV grade services show an increase from 17.55 per cent to 18.32 per cent. In class I service,[20] the position of representation of scheduled castes was as below in Table 64.[20a]

TABLE 64

Showing representation in class I services

In 1963 (Number)	*Percentage*	*In 1968 (Number)*	*Percentage*
239	1.31%	459	2.11%

No Respondent under study has joined any competitive post nor any post through recruitment so far.

The amount spent in the first three plans and proposed in the fourth plan for the welfare of the scheduled castes and backward classes is given below in Table 65 at the All India level.

TABLE 65

Showing outlay for the welfare of the scheduled castes in Five Year Plans

(Rs. in crores)

Sl. No.	*Head*	*I Plan outlay*	*II Plan outlay*	*III Plan outlay*	*IV Plan outlay*
1.	Education	3.88	12.36	24.26	
2.	Economic development	0.25	4.29	4.75	Total outlay for all
3.	Health, housing and other scheme	2.95	10.83	8.90	Scheduled castes 142.42

In the first plan, educational scheme in the state sector were entitled to 75 per cent assistance while other schemes were entitled to 50 per cent assistance. From 1967-68, however, all the schemes in the state sector are entitled to 60 per cent central assistance. In the fourth five year plan, a large allocation of Rs. 134.37 crores has been diverted for the welfare of the scheduled castes minus Doms; Rs. 5 crores have been separately proposed for the Doms.[21]

In the State of Uttar Pradesh, the allocation proposed in respect of various heads of development in the plans[22] has been as follows in the Table 66.

TABLE 66

Showing distribution of proposed outlay in U.P. Plans

(figures in lakhs)

Sl. No.	*Head*	*I Plan*	*II Plan*	*III Plan*	*IV Plan*
1.	Education	213.712	449.850	316.000	309.80
2.	Economic development	34.651	65.990	424.000	126.60
3.	Health, Housing and others	34.587	84.160	190.200	126.50

NOTES AND REFERENCES

1. India 1960, compiled by the Ministry of Information and Broadcasting, Government of India.
2. A study by the Programme Evaluation Organisation, Govt. of India, Planning Commission.
3. Harijan Social Welfare Office, Jaunpur.
   Mr. Usha Rao observes that a large number of scheduled caste students are now going for higher education. In 1973-74 scheduled caste girls alone formed 13.89 per cent after total scheduled caste students as against 27.04 per cent among non-scheduled castes—Deprived castes in India, V 9811 Chugh Publications, Allahabad, p. 339.
4. Briggs. G.W. "The Chamars" (1920). Calcutta Association Press.
5. B.K. Roy Burman observes that adoption of higher education as a means of social uplift has brought about several changes in respect of seven scheduled castes. *viz* , Bawaria, Bhambi, Chamar, Musahar, Parayan, Sansi, Yadava, Social Mobility Movements Among Scheduled Castes and Scheduled Tribes of India, Govt. of India Press, New Delhi. 11, p. 6. B.K. Roy Burman *op. cit.* 14 (in chapter V Occupational Mobility).
6. (i) R.D. Singh: "Social Change in a U.P. Village" For Eastern Quarterly December, 1956.
   (ii) Y. Singh : "Changing Power Structure of Village Community : A Case Study of six villages in Eastern U.P. in Rural Sociology in India" by A.R. Desai, Bombay 1961.
7. R.C. Majumdar : Panchayats in India.
8. (i) Mukerjee. Radhakumud : "Local Goverment in Ancient India", p. 10 (Oxford Clarendon Press, London, 1919).

(ii) Dhillon, H.S. (1955): "Leadership and Groups in a South Indian Village", New Delhi : Planning Commission Programme Evaluation Organisation, Government of India.

9. Oscar, Lewis : Village Life in Northern India, p. 26, Urbana University of Illinois Press, 1958.

10. *Ibid.*,Oscar, Lewis also observes that the panchayats at present have become a forum for the airing of rather trivial disputes between individuals.

11. (i) Prabhat Chandra in Rural leadership in India. The Eastern Anthropologist, September 1959 has also indicated that the upper castes are now trying their best to retain their hold through politicking.

(ii) L.P. Vidyarthi in 'Leadership in India', Asia Publishing House, 1967.

(iii) H. Singh in "Strains in Leadership Structure (from Status-group to Pluralism in an East U.P. Village) in Economic and Political Weekly, May 3, 1969.

12. The development of pluralistic tendencies in the village polity has been also noticed by :

(i) Wildavski who has discussed at length in his work "Leadership in a Small Town", 1964, the salient features of pluralism.

(ii) M.E. Opler in "Factors of Tradition and Change in a local Election in Rural India" cites in his study of Senapur that in the history of the village for the first time, a respected village elder has gone out to seek honour and support rather than to assume that it would accrue to him in due course. (Cited in Leadership and Political Institutions in India by Park and Tinker).

(iii) R. Park & I. Tinker in 'Change in leadership & Political Institutions in India', Oxford, 1970.

13. Quoted in the Times of India, November 18, 1970.

14. David, G. Mandelbaum : "Social Organisation & Planned Culture Change in India", p. 19.

15. Dhillon, H.S. (1955) Leadership and groups in a South Indian village, New Delhi : Planning Commission, Programme Evaluation Organisation, Govt. of India, *op. cit.* p. 127.

16. (i) Salig S. Harrison : "India the most Dangerous Decades", Chapter IV Princeton, 1960.

(ii) Harold R. Issacs : India's Ex-Untouchables, p. 126, Asia Publishing House, Bombay (1965).

17. *Ibid.*, pp. 126-127.

18. See Weber's distinction between power and authority. Authority is legitimised power vested in a particular status or society whereas power is the ability to force, or compel others to do one's will; it is not necessarily legitimised by a particular society. Cf. Weber, Max : Essays in Sociology

translated and edited by H.H. Gerth and C. Wright Mills, New York, Oxford University Press, 1958, pp. 100 and 295.

19. Roy Ramashray : "Congress Defeat in Farrukhabad", (1965) p. 895, Economic Weekly XVII (22).

19a. *Note* : The reserved seats in the state legislatures in 1967 were 503 which increased to 510 in 1971.

20. The Hindustan Times (daily) March 29, 1970.

20a. Representation in Central Services & All India Administrative Services on 1st Jan., 1979 :

Service group	*No. of Hindus*	*Percentage*		*SC*	*ST*
I	43,193	4.50%	IAS	355	160
II	56,095	6.44%	IPS	207	78
III	17,03,729	12.22%	(INDIA—1980)		
IV	12,54,172	19.23%			

21. (i) Five Year Plans.
    (ii) Yojna, April 5, 1970, p. 5.

22. Harijan Welfare in U.P. pp. 16-19 published by the Harijan Social Welfare Directorate, U.P., Lucknow, 1971.

CHAPTER EIGHT

The Scheduled Castes : New Dimensions of Social Change

IN THIS inquiry an attempt has been made to analyse the various facets of the changing socio-economic conditions of the scheduled castes. The findings broadly point to the conclusion that through successive schemes of planning and reform the position of the scheduled castes in the social hierarchy has considerably improved.

Introduction

The scheduled castes which comprise a number of traditionally low order castes have been the virtual underdogs of the Hindu society. They were known as the Shudras and were kept out of the mainstream of Hindu social life. However, with the emergence of modern social forces as a result of India's contact with the West a gradual change started taking place in the attitude of the caste Hindus towards these castes.

After independence and especially after the establishment of democratic republic in India, a number of steps were taken both by the Central and State governments to raise their socio-economic status and towards this end, numerous facilities were extended to them.

The Locale of Interview

There are ten scheduled castes living in the district of Jaunpur in Eastern Uttar Pradesh. For our study we made a pilot survey of those thirteen villages in the district which were selected by the governmental agencies for social welfare activities for the scheduled castes. The castewise break-up of the locale is given in Table 1.

Discussion

In order to appraise the changes that have taken place in the socio-economic conditions of the scheduled castes, we may divide them into the following categories :

1. Social change in respect of social contact, proximity and social outlook
2. Occupational change
3. Economic change (land, industry and trade)
4. Educational and political change
5. Health and sanitation
6. Housing
7. Legal protection and
8. Reservation quota

TABLE 1

Locale of Scheduled Castes in Jaunpur District

Sl. No.	*Name of Caste*	*No. of respondents*	*Villages where the castes dwell (Locale)*
1.	Chamar	140	Kuddupur, Ram Nagar, Khetasarai
2.	Pasi	30	Mahimapur and Ram Nagar
3.	Dhobhi	30	Wazidpur
4.	Musahar	40	Dhanipur
5.	Khatik	30	Jalalpur, Mahimapur and Lalpur
6.	Baheliya	10	Sujanganj and Chak-Gulam-Sarwar
7.	Bansphor (Dharkar)	40	Dhanipur
8.	Nat	20	Taraon
9.	Kanjar (Patharkat)	40	Kheradinganj, Mariyahun
10.	Dom	20	Suburb of the city of Jaunpur

Social Changes

There is gradual realization of self-worth among the scheduled castes. They feel that after independence they have acquired social importance on account of their voting rights. As a result of the numerous facilities being extended to them and the special attention given to them after independence, they have now started leading a life like other free citizens of a democratic country.

They have given up eating beef and removing carcasses and have been keen to wipe out the stigma attached to them of pursuing unclean occupations. In fact, the Chamars in Jaunpur observe commensal taboo on beef. Lynch also reports that the 'Jatwas', a community of Chamars living in the city of Agra have also given up beef.[1] What is the most unusual development is that some scheduled castes have now begun to identify themselves with Kshatriyas and Brahmans. This may be considered as an instance of structural movement for upward mobility which Srinivas calls Sanskritization.[2] However this reference group behaviour solely aims at achieving respectable status in the society but not at assimilation and intermarriage with the group of identification. The informants narrated several legends of how they had descended from an upper caste.

The Chamars, of Jaunpur district style themselves as 'Jaiswars' and consider themselves to be the descendants of Raja Jai Singh. Some educated youths consider their origin as emanating from Ravana, the great king of Sri Lanka. The Pasis claim their origin from Andheriya Kshatriya clan. The Musahars hold that they are the descendants of the Banvasi Raja. The Baheliyas trace their history in the Mahabharata period from Vyadh lineage of Ekalavya. The Bansphors (Dharkars) call themselves descendants of Raja Ben. The Kanjars or stone cutters (Patharkat) speak that they were Bihari Kshatriyas of Sun lineage (Suryavanshi). Towards further enforcing their claim for a better status they are in the process of altering their dress, way of life, education and values. It is also a significant point that their ultimate model of imitation is not the upper caste Hindus, but the westernized man who stands for secularism and conspicuous consumption.[3]

Marriage among them is still arranged by parents. Boys are generally married between 13 and 16 years age while girls are married between 9 and 11 years of age.[4] However 91.75 per cent of the respondents favoured the raising of the age of boys and girls for marriage. Only 8.25 per cent were of the view that no change was required in the age of marriage.

None of the scheduled caste members demonstrated any enthusiasm for the family planning programme. They hold that the programme is associated with 'Nashabandi' and loop etc. which cause permanent lethargy and weakness in men and women.

Untouchability and social distance are still practised by the scheduled castes as well as higher castes. The only change that has come about is that the scheduled caste members are offered seats and served with drinks in the village panchayat meetings, but they are expected even now to sit at a distance from the caste Hindus. Defiling by touch is seldom seen.

The respondents were of the view that economic independence by which they obviously meant a better economic and social status was the best method of liquidating untouchability. The next best was education and the third was social legislation.

Occupational Changes

Regarding occupational change, our study shows that in the father's generation of respondents, only 14 (10 per cent) Chamars started moving from their parental occupations to independent ones. Other scheduled castes did not demontrsate any change at all. In respondent's own generation they exhibited a further tendency for shifting from traditional occupations to new ones. Out of 400 respondents 147 (36.75 per cent) had changed their traditional occupations. Although this departure from the caste based occupations is itself no indication of change, yet it can be easily deduced from this that there is a movement from dependant unskilled occupations to independent ones. This also means that the respondents do have the urge to get into better jobs and are willing to change their present jobs for better ones. Our study also shows that at least 29 out of 140 Chamars under study have given up tanning and taken to service. Tanning is undoubtedly an independent occupation and more lucrative than service. But the Chamar respondents have left it since it was an unclean pursuit which affected their social status; they have forsaken it for a less lucrative but socially more desirable occupation. The only caste which has remained unaffected by the current of change is the Kanjar caste. It is equally important to note that the respondents in the third generation are losing their attraction for agricultural labour and traditional occupations. But they do not show any desire for undertaking an industrial enterprise; they want to go in for trades and business (fruit selling, business in bullocks, pigs and goats). The respondents feel that the present change in their attitudes is on account of their frequent contact with the urban people and sustained interest of the governmental agencies. Their proximity to such influences has been furthered by the rapid growth of means of transport and communication. However, aspiration for better jobs for children is quite high and points to an urge for social climbing. 42.5 per cent respondents under study liked their children to go in for engineering, 15 per cent for the medical line, 11.25 per cent for the PCS cadre. Only 3.5 per cent respondents wished their children to follow their traditional occupation—agriculture. The remaining indicated their likings for other jobs.

Economic Changes

The people under study largely depend on local produce. Their diet hardly provides the essential of nutrition in proper proportion. They frequently consume distilled liquor which has not only deprived the Doms, Chamars, Musahars, Nats, Dhobis and Bansphors, and Kanjars of their savings but has also seriously impaired their health.

A fairly large number of the scheduled castes have been benefitted by the transfer of land under the Zamindari abolition system. This has improved their economic condition and has also made them conscious of their own identity. In consequence the subservient loyalty that they used to owe to the former landlords has declined. The landlords have also become aware of this fact and at some places their mutual relations have become strained.

The progress made in obtaining land through imposition of ceiling on present holdings does not seem to have made any salutary effect on the fate of the scheduled castes. However, the efforts of the government are continuous in this direction. Allotment of lands to landless scheduled castes has been insignificant in the past but now their cases are under consideration at district level. Land collected in *Bhoodan* is being distributed and a number of families are benefitted. The Chamar respondents have shown their eagerness for progress despite their enforced isolation and paucity of resources.

The scheduled castes after having become the owners of their land feel elevated and a sense of belongingness to the land has rapidly grown among them. They now take more interest in their land, its cultivation and crops, etc.

However, the extent of indebtedness among the scheduled castes seems neither alarming nor enormous. In the fathers' generations, they were much affected by indebtednes but in the respondents' own generation, the situation seems to have improved considerably. Only 82.5 per cent are indebted in the present generation while 92.5 per cent were indebted in the fathers' generation. The Doms, Chamars, Dhobis, Musahars, Bansphors (Dharkars), Kanjars and the Nats are indebted mostly on account of their addiction to liquor. Customs of marriage, death and hospitality also force them to take credit.[5] Even today they depend largely upon the local grocer for loans. The reasons are that the grocer extends loan on easy terms. As regards the recovery of loans only 5.25 per cent respondents complained that the money lenders resorted to unscrupulous methods for recovery.

For a satisfactory solution of the unemployment problem, we cannot look to land alone. The area under study has good prospects for the development of certain small-scale-industries, notable among them being consumer goods, industries and processing industries. Palash leaves indusry is one which can be developed sucessfully. Besides, poultry, farming and fishery can also be introduced. Processing of maize, bee-keeping, rope making, net-weaving and soap making have also scope for expansion. These industries can be a secondary source of employment to the scheduled castes who own also lands. For those who have no land, these can be the primary source of employment.

Changes in the Field of Education

There is an upward movement among the respondents in the field of educational attainments. In the grandfathers' generation, their attainments were not even worth-mentioning. However, in the fathers' generation, two fathers (0.5 per cent) had primary education while 398 respondents' fathers (99.50 per cent) had no education at all. This indicates that the tradition of not allowing the scheduled castes in the temples of education, has disappeared. The informants revealed that there was no discrimination against their admission in the primary, junior, higher secondary schools and Universities.

They further revealed that they had no occasion to register any complaint with the authorities about any prejudice. They also admitted that the children were getting scholarships although they were not sufficient in number and amount and not timely either.

The social education classes run by the Harijan Welfare Department or by Community Development Blocks have not played the role that they were expected to play. The respondents reported that no government welfare agencies except malaria units had visited them and attended to their grievances. On account of a similar indifference on the part of other governmental agencies, 79.5 per cent illiteracy still pervades among them. However, some of the respondents regretted their inability to take advantage of these programmes as they had no time to attend such classes even if they were conducted. In the sowing, and harvesting periods, they could not attend the night-classes because they were over-strained due to manual labour in the fields. However, they appreciated the literacy programmes launched for their benefit. The respondents did not show any enthusiasm for women's education. They are afraid that female education will create hindrances in the performance of domestic duties. Assistance to scheduled castes includes grant of stipends, scholarships, freeships, mid-day meals, uniforms, exemption from payment of examination and other fees, book grants and hostel facilities. In the years 1951-52 only 1,604 scheduled castes got post-matric scholarships, but by 1955-56, their number had risen to 78,548. In 1966-67 the number of scholarships awarded, increased further to 90,481. In 1970 Jaunpur district alone registered an increase in the number of scholarships being awarded. The number was 5,631.

Political Changes

The Panchayat Raj and adult franchise have brought in considerable awakening among the scheduled castes under study. They are becoming conscious of their democratic rights. However, there is no visible independent political awareness among them. The educated youths seem to have deflected towards the Arjak Sangh, but not with real earnestness. The respondents usually reposed their confidence in the Congress Party,[6] because it had not only given them ample promises but was also fulfilling them.

In the 1967 general elections, in one constituency the scheduled castes stood behind a Jan Sangh candidate while in another constituency, they threw in their lot with the Congress party. But in the mid-term poll, the loyalties of the Harijans were clustered round the Jan Sangh party, although the victory was equally shared by the Congress and the Jan Sangh parties.

In the election, the respondents favoured those candidates who could manage to procure liquor and other drinks for them or could give them help in the form of cash or promise. 52.6 per cent respondents exercised their right of voting in the general elections held before 1967 while only 47.5 per cent went to the two polls, i.e. 1967 general elections and the mid-term polls held in 1971. 3 respondents (0.75 per cent) out of 400 are working as pradhans of the Gram Sabhas and one respondent (0.25 per cent) is an M.L.A. and another (0.25 per cent) is a Block Pramukh. In the Panchayat sittings they are offered seats and also served with soft drinks. The respondents do not seem to be affiliated to any political party. However, two of their leaders—one from Dhobi caste and another from the Chamar caste are members of the legislative assembly while one Chamar (Jaiswar) is a member of the Lok Sabha.

The caste Hindus have now started looking at them as their legitimate competitors and, thus, they try consciously to retain their hold through politicking. The upper castes who used to be the leaders of the polity and who obtained the support of the lower castes through sheer dominance and influence, have now revised their thinking. This development points to the evolution of pluralistic tendencies in the village polity.

The formal institutions have not, however, been able to do away with the popularity and sanctity of informal institutions, notably the caste Panchayats. They even today regulate the moral conduct of the members of a community. They set limits to dowry and to the number of persons to participate in a marriage party. They also arrange return of wives who have deserted their husbands.

Changes in the field of Health and Sanitation

One of the prime necessities for the better upkeep of man is the provision of safe drinking water. Most of the diseases can be attributed to contaminated water. Water facilities available to the scheduled castes are by no means adequate. The Musahars and Bansphors of Dhanipur (Jaunpur), Nats of Taraon Village are experiencing considerable scarcity of drinking water. Their demand is even today, unfulfilled.

The welfare agencies should meet their demand as early as possible. The government of Uttar Pradesh provides Rs. 1000 for the construction of a well as grants-in-aid. The arrangement for the rest of the money is to be made by the parties concerned. For a hand pump the amount granted is Rs. 220. It is slackness on the part of the scheduled castes that they have not availed of these assistance programmes.

At each step the government cannot be blamed. Bringing health services within the reach of all and improving the standard of national health are not easy tasks by any means. They require steadiness on the part of the government, as patience on the part of the people. The National Tuberculosis Control Programme and the National Malaria Control Programme, Mass Veneral Disease Treatment Campaign and the Leprosy Control Scheme have entered into their major operational phase throughout the length and breadth of the country. The scheduled castes under study have greatly appreciated the anti-malaria campaign. The National water and sanitation programme has not undertaken the welfare work in the district of Jaunpur as yet. Side by side, a considerable number of maternity establishments and health centres are needed in the district.

Housing

Sufficient funds are sanctioned for the construction of houses for scheduled castes both in urban and rural areas. In the district of Jaunpur, colonies for certain castes have been constructed. The Kanjars, Doms and Chamars of Kheradinganj and Khetasarai are now living in their colonies. But many Dom families are still living in slums. The government of India, Ministry of Works, Housing and Supply provides adequate financial assistance to State government and through them to municipal and local bodies for the clearance of slum areas. The financial aspect of assistance is 37.5 per cent of the approved cost as outright subsidy in metropolitan cities, 37.5 per cent as loan by the Centre and the remaining 25 per cent is to be borne by the State government.

The village housing scheme of the Ministry of Works, Housing and Supply during the Second Five Year Plan was expected to cover 5,000 villages all over the country. Besides, detailed technical advice and guidance is provided free of cost to the villagers by the Rural Housing Cells—a field staff under the Block authorities.[7] None of the scheduled caste members have availed of such advice. Funds in the form of subsidy are provided to the Doms for the procurements of long boots, long brooms and moving latrines (Japanese type latrines). It is very much astounding to note that no Dom family has tried to avail itself of the facility. Reasons : first, they are actually not aware of these facilities and second, they are shy of pressing their problems for immediate settlement. Third, they rather avoid going to the authorities on account of their inferiority complex.

Legal Protection and Change

Legislative and executive measures, in respect of land tenure, fundamental rights, social justice and education have been enforced to safeguard the interests of scheduled castes in the various States. The Zamindari Abolition Act, the Untouchability Act 1955 and the Acts of 1955 and 1956 on marriage and inheritance have further strengthened the rights of the scheduled castes. Our findings in this regard are that under Untouchability Offences Act 1955, no person was arrested. *Begari* has vanished, although *Harwahi Pratha* has replaced it. No specific steps have been taken to protect the scheduled castes from exploitation by money-lenders. At present, the Government of Uttar Pradesh has taken hasty steps to erase the baneful effects of lending money.

Reservation Quota

Despite reservation quota in all Central and State government services, the scheduled castes under study have not been able to get into either of them. However, they aspire for better jobs for their children. Nirmal Kumar Bose, the former Commissioner for Scheduled Castes and Scheduled Tribes in his annual report for 1969, presented the following recommendations for the speedy development of scheduled castes in various fields :

1. Appointment of lady social workers for effective propaganda.
2. Weaning away of the scheduled castes from traditional caste based occupations.

3. Increase of reservation quota upto 50 per cent i.e. 50 per cent vacancies should be reserved.
4. Setting up of co-operative societies for scavangers for their economic development.[8]

However, these recommendations have not been accepted so far by the government. There is, however, every possibility of the proposal regarding reservation quota being opposed by the general public since it takes away a large slice of the services from the deserving and meritorious.

The question may arise whether the special privileges granted to scheduled castes tended to foster security, self-pride and self-independence among them ? There is no doubt that such facilities and special privileges have enabled them the better to solve their problems and have also been benefiting their children.[9]

Depending so much on government initiative, the scheduled castes will be isolated from the mainstreams of life and their personal initiative will be killed. R. Achutan is right when he maintains that the Harijan leaders have acquired a vested interest in keeping the untouchables backward and isolated from the mainstream of Hindu life. He sounded the warning that if Harijans themselves wanted to remain Harijans for ever their uplift will for ever remain an illusion.[10] The official agencies have no doubt an important role to play in securing the integration of the scheduled castes with the upper castes of the Hindu society without disturbing their essential harmony of life. But it should not be forgotten that unless the former are themselves prepared to share the new responsibilities according to their capacities, no real advancement can take place in their position.

There is, however, no denying the fact that legislations and recommendations alone cannot take us very far unless we are able to carry public opinion with us. The canker of untouchability will take time to disappear. However, this is an accepted fact that the legal guarantees now available to them have paved entirely a new way for the scheduled castes. The distinction between the cultural and structural dimensions of caste appears to be minimised. Untouchability stands abolished under law and its practice in any form is forbidden.[11]

NOTES AND REFERENCES

1. Lynch, O.M. 1969, *The Politics of Untouchability, A case from Agra, India* Columbia University Press, New York and London.

2. Srinivas, M.N. 1962, "Changing Institution and Values in Modern India" *Economic Weekly, Annual Review*, February.

3. In his opinion K. Ranga Rao also observes : As Sanskritization largely failed to meet the rising aspirations of the low castes to gain status mobility, contact with the West during the British era brought about another kind of social change : Westernization which promised better economic opportunities to enhance class if not caste mobility, cf. Ranga Rao : "Rural Leadership & Conflct (Study of an Andhra Village)", *Economic and Political Weekly* Vol. III, No. 17, April 27, 1967 p. 675. However our findings are different from those of K.L. Sharma: cf. Stresses in Caste Stratification —A study of six villages". *Economic and Political Weekly*, Vol. IV No. 3 Jan. 18, 1969, p. 222. According to Sharma the lower castes consider obsolete and outdated. The upper castes modernise their life styles in a way which is beyoned the reach of the lower castes.

4. Benard Cohn in *The Chamars of Senapur (Jaunpur)*, 1954 unpublished Ph.D. dissertation, also cites the age of marriage among the Chamars as between 13 years and 16 years (boys) and 8 years & 10 years (girls).

5. (i) The special Assistant Agent, Bhandrachalam gave the following causes for indebtedness among the scheduled castes and scheduled tribes; meagre income due to infertile land, ignorance of equitable price system, adherence to panchayat (caste panchayats) decisions and payment of fines imposed by them and social celebrations at large scale (quoted in *Report of the Scheduled Castes and Scheduled Tribes Commission* Vol. I, 1960-61 p. 200). (ii) See also the *Report of the Commissioner for Scheduled Castes and Scheduled Tribes* for the year 1959-60.

6. Cohn (1954 : 171-72) on the other hand notes that the Chamars of Senapur village have become disillusioned with the Congress and call it a bad party. Yet no other party has come to take its place. *The Chamars of Senapur : A study of the Changing status, of a Depressed Caste*, Cornell University, 1954. (Uupublished Ph.D. dissertation).

7. *Report of the Commissioners for Scheduled Castes and Scheduled Tribes* (1959-60), p. 170.

8. *Annual Report on Scheduled Castes and Tribes* presented on 15 May, 1969 by Nirmal Kumar Bose.

9. T.K. Oommen also records that special privileges extended to the weaker sections in society including the untouchables were intended to emancipate the castes; but instead they have created caste consciousness all around. The middle castes feel their superiority threatened when more and more of the lower castes improve their economic lot making them economically independent of rich landlords and cultivators who form the middle castes.

cf. : "Strategy for Social Change (A study of Untouchability)" *Economic and Political Weekly*, Vol. III No. 25, June 22, 1968 p. 935.

10. R. Achutan, A member of the Untouchability Committee 1965. His remarks appeared in the *Report of the Committee on Untouchability*, April 1969.

11. Marc Galanter also observes that the sacral view of caste has been drastically impaired on account of the constitutional commitments to social traformation. The scheduled castes can now freely make use of the legal resources if they feel insecure anywhere. They have legal protection for advancing their claims for recognition. The judiciary has been playing the role of a mediator between the aspirations of scheduled castes and their activities in society. Marc Galanter, "Changing Legal Conception of Caste" (A paper prepared on Religion and Politics in South India held in Colombo in July, 1964), and "Law and Caste in Modern India", *Asian Survey* III (ii) 1963 pp. 544 & 559.

CHAPTER NINE

A Study of Intercaste Relations and Social Distance Among Scheduled Castes

Introduction

IN INDIA there has been a welcome awakened interest in carrying out studies in the field of social distance and intercaste relations among scheduled castes after independence. However, studies published thus far make it clear that there is still much factual information to be obtained as there are, even today, several issues to be settled which need special and thorough probe. In rural India intercaste relations studies have been undertaken only with a view to ascertaining the role of education, occupation power, income and out-group as determinants of social strata in the context of social change. There is now extensive literature available on the subject.

Problem

In this enquiry an attempt has been made to analyse the existing pattern of intercaste relations and social distance in the form untouchability among scheduled castes with special reference to Jaunpur district in eastern Uttar Pradesh, India. The universe consists of 400 respondents drawn from ten scheduled castes inhabiting the district. The castes are: Chamar, Dom, Dhobi, Musahar, Pasi, Bansphor, (Dharkar), Kanjar, Nat, Khatik and Baheliya. The field investigation was conducted in thirteen villages—Kuddupur, Ram Nagar, Mahimapur, Jalalpur, Lalpur,

Khetasarai, Kheradingani, Taraon Chak gulam Sarwar, Wazidpur, Dhanipur, Sujanganj and the suburb of Jaunpur city. The villages were covered more or less by social welfare programmes launched by the state.

Method

The respondents under study do not constitute a sample, but a population. The study has an exploratory design, and is based on primary data which were collected through the help of an interview schedule combined with participant observation.

Discussion

Social distance implies a differential reaction to the various groups in the community. It also refers to subordination and superordination. Park defines it as grades and degrees of understanding and intimacy which characterise presocial and social relations generally.[1] Johnson observes that if members of two different social strata come to have intimate social relationships there would develop among them a sense of mutual acceptability as equals or near equals. If the members of two social groups maintain social distance and interest as unequals, they would avoid and, even, resist social relationships with each other.[2]

The traditional pattern of social interactions between the scheduled castes and the caste Hindus reflects the idea of pollution and social distance. Social distance has manifested itself in the form of untouchability in India. After independence the speedy liquidation of untouchability has been the declared policy of the state and its practice is now punishable under law. The scheduled castes observe strict rules of pollution even amongst themselves. A sheikhda (a sub-caste of Dom) does not accept food at the hands of hela Dom although both are the offshoots of one and the same caste. Contact between a Chamar and a Dom is considered to be defiling. They do not practise interdinning either with the caste Hindus or among themselves. A washerman never interdines with a Khatik nor a Baheliya intermarries with a Kanjar girl. As to the existing pattern of intercaste relations, 15 per cent scheduled castes favoured intercaste relations and 85 per cent, except for the use of drinking water wells, were not willing to have social interactions with higher castes on the basis of equality. Regarding matrimonial alliance, with higher castes or among themselves they were by and large unwilling.[3] Reasons: one, they want to preserve their own identity as distinct social groups deserving special privileges presently enjoyed by them under various legislative and administrative provision,[4] two, they cannot do all these things because cultural adjustments will become difficult; three, they have district origins and hence do not like to tarnish the horary past traditions.

The scheduled castes, however, meet on certain festivals, such as; Holi in the anchayat meetings. They are offered seats during the meetings of the political bodies. 0.75 per cent respondents, who were also pradhans, indicated that they were offered seats, but at a distance from the caste Hindus. Smokes and drinks were also offered to them in earthen rather than brasswares, and the remaining 99.25 per cent stated that they were served food etc. in the homes of caste Hindus in pattals made of palash tree leaves. Now as regards social distance, our findings are that there is no change in the traditional practice. Democratization has, of course, compelled the cast Hindus to relent their attitude to some extent but in their heart of hearts they still nurse the same feeling of distance. And why to single out the caste Hindus, the scheduled castes themselves continue to maintain distance as among themselves.[4]

The closed and simple nature of the rural society gives the various castes ample freedom and scope to observe norms strictly. Traditionally the scheduled castes were not allowed to enter the temples. There is no change in the situation even now. The scheduled castes are not permitted to worship at the temples maintained by the caste Hindus. The respondents, in this connection were of the view that they could not hide their caste identity nor would they be bold enough to enter temples. 82.25 per cent respondents admitted that if they tried to do odd acts (acts of entering temples) they would be shown their places, do while 14.75 per cent, however, accepted that they could have a darshan of deities in temples and offer their prayers, but from a distance.[5]

In the rural areas, the scheduled castes have generally got their own wells. They frequently make use of the river ghats, canals and no caste Hindu has shown any indignation towards them while they have their bath. However they did not mention any case of indiscrimination regarding admission to the rural and urban schools.

As far as the change of caste is concerned, they still cherish that human beings cannot change anybody's castes. They cannot raise their voices against the evil practice since they are themselves economically dependent on others and nobody will care to listen to them. That is why they do not protest against untouchability from within and from without the caste.[6]

However 34.50 per cent scheduled castes were of the view that liquidation of untouchability could be made alone by the extension of education among them, 12.75 per cent maintained that legislation could liquidate while 52.75 per cent advanced that economic independence was the surest way of killing, it. Thus, majority of the scheduled castes hold the view that their economic independence by which they obviously mean a better economic and social status is the best method of liquidating untouchability. The next best is education and third is social legislations.

Whether the services of the barbers and washermen were available to them, 5 per cent Dom respondents indicated that the washermen were not serving them, but barbers were rendering their services. In rural India, the scheduled castes have their own castemen who serve them. The priests visit their houses on request and they superwise their rituals and accept their fees, but do not take meals at their places. In lieu of meals, they accept flour, pulse money and clothes from them and generally cook by themselves.

Conclusion

Untouchability and social distance are still practised by the scheduled castes as well as higher castes. The only change that has come about is that the scheduled caste members are now offered seats and served with soft drinks in the village panchayat meetings, but they are expected to sit, even at a distance from the caste Hindus. However, none of the scheduled castes, mentioned about any indiscrimination regarding admission to the rural and urban schools.[7]

In independent India they feel better than before and have rather developed a feeling of self assertion and have, also, been able to establish their own identity in social spectrum. They agree that their position has acquired a social importance on account of their voting rights and reservation quota in the political bodies.

The influence of new legislations and education has resulted in secularising and liberalizing the attitudes of both the scheduled castes and the caste Hindus. The caste Hindus have, also, oriented the past values to new situations.[8] Psychic factors play, still a, dominating part in perpetuating the canker of untouchability. The canker of untouchability will take time to disappear. Moreover, it will depend upon the participation of Harijans in the process of achievements in the field of education, wealth and political power.[9]

NOTES AND REFERENCES

1. Park, R.E. : The Concept of Social Distance Jn. of Appl. Soc., 1923.
2. Henry Johnson : Sociology : A systematic Introduction, Indian Edition, 1966, Bombay Allied Publishers, p. 504.
3. A. Bopegamage & P.V. Veerraghawan in their work *'Status Images in Changing India* (Bombay, Manaktola, 1967) also indicate that the untouchables enjoy lower acceptability as compared to other castes.

   (ii) H.S. Bhatia also in his article *'Intercaste Relations and Aspirational Levels*—An Attitude study appeared in *Indian Journal of Social Work* Vol. XXXI No. 1, April, 1970 says that the Harijans do not seem to be willing to have social interactions on equality basis in great measure.
4. Aiyappan, A. in Social Revolution in Kerala Village—A Study in Culture Change (1965), *The Iravas—An Untouchable Cast in Kerala* (Bombay) maintains that with greater awareness of their political significance and the emergence of vested interests within their communities, the tendency for preserving their identity is likely to become more apparent.
5. Taya Zinkin in a Tanjore village remarks that in a Tanjore village, the Harijan himseif would probably not try to enter a caste shrine and if he did, the village castes would probably soon bring him to heel, law or no law.

   (ii) G.N. Ramu in 'Hosure Village : Untouchability in Rural Areas : *Indian Journal of Social Work* Vol. XXIX No. 2 July 1968 observes that Hosure villagers believe that caste is owing to sins committed in the previous birth, because they believe that such acts pollute the village deities. If the village deity is polluted they are bound to suffer all sorts of incurable diseases.
6. Dube, S.C. in Indian Villages p. 224.

   (i) Routledges Kegan Paul, 1965 observes that the untouchables are careful not to voice their protests so loudly or publicly for they are conscious of the advantages of silence in view of their dependent position in the economic structure of the community.

   (ii) Srinivas, M.N. in his study : *'Caste in Modern India and other Essays* p. 104 maintains as long as the Harijans are not economically independent of the Higher castes, the rights which the constitution guarantees will not be translated into practice.

7. Nineth Report of the Commissioner for scheduled castes and Tribes section V pp. 29-30 for 1959-1960, also says that untouchability in U.P., Rajasthan (51 villages covered) Gujarat and Maharashtra varies considerably from village to village and the intolerant practices are waning out fast. Cases of indiscrimination are rare.

8. A.L. Srivastava in his article 'Attitude towards Harijans yet to change'. *Social Welfare*, October, 1970 p. 11 states that more often the feeling has gone to the extent of arrogance and rebellion against Caste Hindus.

9. H.S. Bhatia also observes in his article 'Intercaste Relations & Aspirational Levels Vol. No. XXXI. No. 1 *Indian Journal of Social Work* April 1970 that achievement dimensions of social status by Harijans will largely affect the mode of interaction with Caste Hindus.

CHAPTER TEN

The Changing Socio-Economic Conditions of the Scheduled Castes in District Jaunpur, U.P.

The Problem

THE ABOVE WORK is a study on the changing socio-economic conditions of the scheduled castes with special reference to Jaunpur district in eastern Uttar Pradesh. The aim is to assess the changes that have taken place in the life of the scheduled castes as a result of the socio-political changes in India in recent years.

Methodology

The enquiry was made in thirteen villages which were selected by the government agencies for extension of welfare programmes. The villages include Kuddupur, Ram Nagar, Mahimapur, Jalalpur, Lalpur, Sujanganj, Chak-gulam Sarwar, Wazidpur, Taraon, Kheradinganj, Khetasarai, Dhanipur and the suburbs of Jaunpur city. Four hundred respondents were drawn for substantiating the enquiry from ten scheduled castes living in these villages. The castes are Chamar, Pasi, Khatik, Dom, Nat, Dhobi, Kanjar, Bansphor, (Dharkar), Musahar and Baheliya. The study has an exploratory design, and is mainly based on primary data collected through the help of an interview schedule combined with participant observation. Besides, sufficient use of secondary data has also been made.

The scheduled castes covered can be grouped under three broad occupational divisions: (1) the agriculturists who own land and cultivate the land (Pasis, Baheliyas and few Chamars), (2) the craftsmen who follow certain trades (Musahar, Bansphor, Nat, Kanjar, Khatik and Dhobi), and (3) the labourers who work on daily wages (some Pasis, Chamars and Doms).

Findings

Economic Conditions

The respondents on the whole appear to be economically better off than before. Despite the decline in the value of the rupee in the course of years, their standard of living—food and drink, house and health—seems to be higher than that of their forefathers, one or two generations ago.

There is a slow but steady change in the occupations of these castes from dependent unskilled occupations to independent ones. Agriculture is no longer their only field as they take more interest in white-coller jobs. Out of 400 respondents, 36.75 per cent have adopted occupations other than their traditional ones while 63.25 per cent still stick to their traditional occupations. Such changes are due to their frequent contact made easier by rapid means of communication and transport with urban people and various governmental agencies who approach them for different purposes.

Indebtedness among the scheduled castes does not appear to be as alarming or enormous as it was before independence. The reasons for indebtedness are meagre income, addiction to liquor, heavy expenditure on marriage, death ceremonies, etc.

The living conditions of the scheduled castes continue to be miserably poor in certain respects. Their diet hardly provides the essential nutrition in proper proportion. Anaemia is not uncommon amongst them. Minor and major ailments affect the economic position of the individual and the group. Addiction to distilled liquor, common among the Doms, Chamars, Musahars, Nats, Dhobis, Bansphors, and Kanjars, has seriously impaired their health and has deprived them of their small savings.

The scheduled castes are also in need of land for cultivation. The housing scheme started by the government has encouraged these castes to look to the government to do everything for them thereby reducing their self-reliance. In some cases, the benefits of this programme have gone to the well-to-do among them who may be owing a house already. The really deserving poor Nats, Musahars and the Bansphors derive no benefit as they are unable to pay their contribution in cash. Moreover, the houses built under the government scheme have a weak structure and the people living in them feel insecure. The government of Uttar Pradesh has drawn up a tentative scheme for construction of over 2,000 quarters for scheduled caste employees by granting subsidies, to the municipal boards.

Social Conditions

Familism is still a governing factor in the settlement of marriage among these castes. No one favours marriage by choice of the boys and girls. They are against intercaste marriage, but do not object to it if it takes place. They favour the raising of the age of marriage for both boys and girls.

Democratization has, of course, compelled the caste Hindus to relent their attitude towards the scheduled castes to some extent, but in their heart of hearts they still nurse the same feelings of distance.

The scheduled castes themselves continue to maintain distance among themselves. The only change that has come about is that the scheduled caste members are now offered seats and served with drinks in the village panchayat meetings. There is no discrimination regarding admission to the rural and urban schools. There is no practice of beggary anywhere, but *Harwahi Pratha*, the system of engaging scheduled castes for menial work such as tilling the land and looking after cattle on monthly or annual payment or for repayment of old debts still exists. Their model of imitation is not the upper caste Hindus, but the westernised Hindus who stand for secularism and a higher life. A preponderant majority of them, 92.5 per cent, prefer being called Harijans; 1 per cent only want complete deletion of the term Harijan and 6.5 per cent prefer to be called the scheduled castes.

Literacy among the scheduled castes on the whole is much than lower the general percentage of literacy in the country. The percentage of literates among the scheduled castes is estimated to be 6.5. But in Uttar Pradesh, 20.9 per cent of the total population of the scheduled castes are now having higher eduation. Among the respondents of this study, 78.5 per cent are literate, and even the wholesale eradication of illiteracy among scheduled castes is not an impossibility. Every year, nearly about 2,800 young men belonging to the scheduled castes obtain their Bachelor's Degree. A large number of the educated young men of these castes are moving into government jobs, mostly in the lower clerical grades. In the near future, education may, therefore, make a big impact on their thinking and action.

Panchayati Raj and extension of adult franchise have legitimatized the leadership aspirations of the scheduled castes. Both theoretically and practically they can now participate in the rural and urban polity on an equal footing. In most of the general elections they have exercised their franchise. In three villages under study they are represented in three *gaon* panchayats through their elected *pradhans*.

In the near future, the scheduled castes may assert their numerical strength for political power. But, at present they are not united because of their diverse social background. There is no visible sign of independent political thinking among them. They inform that they would support the Congress Party as long as they are taken care of. The traditional panchayats will exercise judicial functions and regulate moral conduct among the scheduled castes.

General Changes

There is no doubt that the facilities and special privileges granted to Harijans have redressed many of their grievances and have benefited their children. But there is a danger that such dependency on government initiative may isolate the Harijans from the mainstream of Hindu life and may kill their initiative.

No doubt, there are many changes occurring in the life of the scheduled castes under the pressure of new situations. Notable among the factors which are responsible for the socio-economic transformation of these castes are the welfare programmes, new transportation facilities, the growing political worth of these castes, and the increasing awareness among them. The land settlement schemes, new social legislations and the various constitutional provisions for their welfare have gone a long way towards removing their disabilities.

The Untouchability Committee's recommendations (submitted in 1969) regarding the establishment of a Finance Corporation for providing financial help to the scheduled caste members is indeed very sound. It has been emphasized by the Committee that Finance Corporations should be able to play a big role in improving the economic conditions of the Harijans.

The present study has thrown light on the need for special studies on the education, health, housing and economic development of the scheduled castes and for exploring the impact of development and the Harijan welfare programmes.

CHAPTER ELEVEN

Indebtedness of Scheduled Castes

AN ATTEMPT is made here to analyze the magnitude of indebtedness among the scheduled castes with particular reference to Jaunpur District in eastern Uttar Pradesh, which is noted for its poverty, growing pressure of population, low level of literacy and unemployment. Incidentally, Jaunpur was one of the districts surveyed by the Patel Commission appointed by the Government of India to enquire into the backwardness of eastern Uttar Pradesh.

Area of Research and Methodology

The note is based on field work done in over a dozen of villages, namely Kuddupur, Ram Nagar, Mahimapur, Dhanipur, Wazidpur, Lalpur, Jalalpur, Sujanganj, Chal-gulam sarwar, Kheradinganj, Khetasarai, Taraon and the suburb of Jaunpur city. All the villages were more or less covered by the government welfare programmes. In all 400 respondents representing ten scheduled castes, namely Chamar, Dom, Kanjar, Nat, Pasi, Khatik, Baheliya, Bansphor (Dharkar), Musahar and Dhobi were interviewed.

Magnitude of Indebtedness

In order to assess the magnitude of indebtedness in the country, a general survey was carried out in the year 1954 under government auspices, but the observations and recommendations did not relate specifically to the scheduled castes. It was only in 1961 that the

Registrar General of India published the statewise extent of indebtedness among the scheduled castes (Table 1), which showed that

TABLE 1

Distribution of Indebtedness of Scheduled Castes in Different States

Name of State	*Percentage of the scheduled caste families under debt*	
	Rural	*Urban*
Andhra Pradesh	69.66%	49.41%
Assam	47.51%	20.40%
Bihar	65.99%	54.49%
Gujarat	45.24%	54.64%
Jammu & Kashmir	52.69%	16.45%
Kerala	60.61%	46.82%
Madhya Pradesh	65.46%	41.06%
Tamil Nadu	65.33%	57.75%
Maharashtra	48.69%	44.78%
Karnataka (Mysore)	65.52%	61.22%
Orissa	49.38%	24.07%
Punjab	63.84%	44.20%
Rajasthan	61.14%	63.79%
Uttar Pradesh	62.55%	50.27%
West Bengal	55.25%	22.83%
Central Areas	78.56%	65.06%

in Uttar Pradesh 62.55 per cent and 50.27 per cent of the scheduled caste families were under debt in the villages and urban areas respectively. The study of indebtedness in two generations of the scheduled castes revealed two facts : first, the degree of indebtedness had decreased over the two generations; second, Chamar respondents' fathers were most heavily indebted; next came the fathers of Doms, Nats, Bansphors, Musahars, Dhobis, Khatiks, Kanjars and Pasis in that order while Baheliya respondents' fathers were free from indebtedness. But in the respondents' generation, the order seems to have changed : The Khatik, Pasi and Baheliya respondents indicated that they were no longer under debt whereas Chamars, Doms, Dhobis, Musahars, Bansphors, Nats, and Kanjars were no doubt under debt, but the enormity of debt was not alarming (Table 2).

TABLE 2

Extent of Indebtedness per Family

Name of Caste	*Fathers' generation debt in Rs.*	*Respondents' generation debt in Rs.*
Dom	450 to 700	200 to 300
Chamar	650 to 900	300 to 375
Kanjar	200 to 300	170
Musahar	400 to 450	200 to 250
Bansphor	300 to 500	120 to 200
Nat	450 to 600	100 to 150
Dhobi	300 to 500	200 to 300
Khatik	350 to 400	Nil
Pasi	150 to 200	Nil
Baheliya	Nil	Nil

Causes of Indebtedness

Our study has revealed the following causes of indebtedness of the scheduled castes : (1) They are either landless or have very small pieces of land of poor quality. (2) The religious, convivial and habitual use of liquor as a result of which major part of their income is squandered away on drinks. (3) They are forced to celebrate their festivities with pomp and show by their own community, failing which they are fined by their caste panchayats. For fear of ex-communication and heavy fines, they comply with the expectations of their community and caste panchayats.

Sources of Borrowing Money

As to the sources of borrowing money, the respondents indicated the following sources : (1) Professional money lenders; (2) agriculturist money lenders; (3) Government agencies; (4) relatives; and (5) muqadam of the village. As many as 78.5 per cent respondents indicated that they borrowed money from the village grocer. Whether the money lenders resorted to some unscrupulous means of recovery of dues, 5.25 per cent respondents narrated that they paid towards redemption of their debt, but to their surprise their regular payment was counted against interest and the capital borrowed, thus, always remained unpaid. Twenty respondents (5 per cent) stated that the position of the money-lenders or *sahukar* was impregnable on account of the absence of an alternative source of easy credit. They said that they joined a co-operative society in a neighbouring village and deposited their shares in it but later it was discovered that the total assets of the society were misappropriated and the society was declared a defunct body by its president.

Socio-Cultural Obstacles

Those who have neither land nor any substantial occupation are the worst affected. The development schemes have not affected every class equally and the lot of the scheduled castes still leaves much to be desired. But there are social obstacles also in the way of their development. When suggested that they should start poultry farm, fishery or piggary for augmenting their income their blanket answer was that they would rather die than contaminate their religion by adopting these trades. Apart from major and effective land reforms, it is essential to remove such socio-cultural obstacles to pave the way for the development of cottage industries and diversification of economic activity. The local leaders can do a lot in this regard.

CHAPTER TWELVE

Weaker Sections in India and Reform Movements

THE IMAGE of the weaker-sections of the society is usually conveyed in India through the social groups labelled "The Scheduled Castes and Tribes." The juridical category of the scheduled castes and tribes does not identify comprehensively and precisely the weaker sections of the society. The fact is that an appreciable number of those belonging to these groups are doing well in the economic and political sphere in contemporary India. It was during the British rule that attempts were made by the English educated intelligentia to do away with the restrictions prevailing in the caste system and to assimilate the untouchables into the fold of higher Hinduism, Raja Ram Mohan Ray, Keshava Chandra Sen and Devendra Nath Tagore founded the Brahmo Samaj and through it established a brotherhood wherein members will not be divided on the caste basis. The Prārthanā Sāmāj also gave a jolt to the old Hindu traditions and institutions. M.G. Ranade, Chandavarkar, Bhandarkar and Agarkar were the pioneers who stood for remodelling the Hindu society. The 'Deo Sāmāj' led by Siva Nārāyān Agnihotri was very similar to that of the Brahmo Sāmāj.

In 1875, Swami Daya Nand established the Arya Samaj with a view to reconstructing the Hindu Society. The accomplish his splendid dream, he dealt heavy blows at the accumulated superstitions of the centuries and the Brahmanical church as did Luther at the Roman church. His ideal was to see India rejuvenated and revitalized socially religiously and politically. He suggested character, action and nature as the criteria of caste.

The Theosophical Society led by Mrs. Annie Besant also decried the obscurantist practices of Hindu society and pleaded for a synthesis of the East and the West. Other militant movements against the rigid order of caste were led by Jyotir Phooley and A. B. Lathe, Shinde and A.V. Thakkar. The Vaikam Movement of 1924 manifested a determined effort of the depressed classes in Kerala. In 1925, the Madras legislative council introduced a bill which threw open all public schools to all classes of people.

Inspite of the many movements organised by religious and political leaders and legal measures adopted by the government, the position of the scheduled castes had altered very little until the dawn of independence.

Independence brought many promises for these people in the field of politics. A number of provisions were incorporated in the new Indian constitution for the protection of Harijans. The appointment of a Commissioner for scheduled castes and scheduled tribes to look after the interests and welfare of these people was a landmark in the history of the country.

The Untouchability Act 1955, the Protection of Civil Rights Act, 1976 and special provisions in the VIth Five Year Plan and now in the VIIth Five Year Plan Draft have strengthened the rights of the Harijans for social utilities.

Besides the efforts being made by the voluntary agencies like Harijan Sewak Sangh, Bhartiya Depressed Classes League and Bharat Dalit Sewak Sangh are, also, commendable.

The Dalit Literary Movement (DLM) in Maharashtra is purely a literary movement and through its various periodicals it is reaffirming the solidarity of Harijans and rejuvenating their ideological commitments and helping in formulating their further policies and strategies.

Chapter Thirteen

Summary and Conclusion

In the foregoing chapters we have analysed the various facets of the changing socio-economic conditions of the scheduled castes. Our findings broadly point to the conclusion that through successive schemes of planning and reform the position of the scheduled castes in the social hierarchy has considerably improved. In order to appraise the changes that have taken place in their socio-economic conditions we may divide them into the following categories:

1. Social changes in respect of social contact, proximity and social outlook,
2. Occupational change,
3. Economic changes (land, industry and trade),
4. Education, and political change,
5. Health and sanitation,
6. Housing,
7. Legal protection, and
8. Reservation quota.

Social Change

There is gradual realization of self worth among the scheduled castes. They feel that after independence they have acquired social importance on account of their voting rights. As a result of the numerous facilities being extended to them and the special attention given to them after independence they have now started behaving like free citizens of a democratic country.

They have given up eating beef and removing carcasses and have been keen to wipe out the stigma attached to them of pursuing unclean occupations. In fact the Chamars in Jaunpur observe commensal taboo on beef. Lynch also reports that the Jatwas a community of Chamars living in the city of Agra have also given up beef. What is a most unusual development is that some scheduled castes have now begun to identify themselves with Kshatriyas and Brahmans. This may be considered as an instance of structural movement for upward mobility, what Srinivas calls Sanskritization. However, this reference group behaviour solely aims at achieving of respectable status in the society not at assimilation and inter-marriage with the group of identification. The informants narrated several legends of how they had descended from an upper caste. Towards further enforcing their claim for a better status they are in the process of altering their dress, way of life, education and values. It is also a significant point that their ultimate model of imitation, is not the upper caste Hindus but the westernised man who stands for secularism and conspicuous consumption.

Marriage among them is still an economic and social ceremony. Parents consider it their most pious duty to arrange the marriage of their children. The majority of the respondents favoured the raising of the age of boys and girls. Only a small percentage was of the view that no change was required in the age of marriage. All the castes insist on marrying their sons and daughters within their own caste. They are against intercaste marriage, but do not object to it if it takes place. However with changing social set up several modern forces are contributing to the modification of their institution. The recent social legislation on marriage and inheritance and the growing influence of urbanization have led to a general awareness and realization of social equality on the part of the scheduled castes.

The joint family based on the practice of living together bound by marriage and common purse has been an all pervading institution. 70 per cent respondents are still within the precincts of joint family while only 30 per cent have nuclear families. This change may be described as a shift from the institutionalism of joint family to the personalism of the nuclear family.

Family traditions still govern the behaviour of the scheduled castes, apart the elders in the family even today play the role of informal family counsellors. None of the scheduled castes under study has shown any enthusiasm for the family planning programme. They still believe that the progeny is the blessing of God. However, they agree that the programme is very much helpful in restricting the family in size and in preserving the family welfare.

Democratisation has compelled the caste. Hindus to change their attitude to some extent towards the Harijans, but in their hearts they still nourish the feeling of social distance. And why single out the caste Hindus, the scheduled castes themselves continue to maintain social distance even among themselves. It was observed that the Hela Doms did not accept food at the hands of Doms, such as Sheikhda. However, defiling by touch was seldom seen.

Our respondents were of the view that their economic independence by which they obviously meant a better economic and social status was the best method of liquidating untouchability. The next best was education and third was social legislation.

92.5 per cent preferred being named Harijans while 6.5 per cent preferred being called scheduled castes.

Occupational Change

Our study shows that the respondents in their fathers' generation had started moving from their parental to other occupations that is to say from dependant occupations of agricultural labourers to independent occupations such as traders like tanning of leather. In the fathers' generation 14 Chamars out of 140 (10 per cent) had changed their fathers' occupation but the other scheduled castes did not adopt any change. In their own generation, however, the respondents have shown a farther tendency for shifting from agricultural labour and traditional occupations to new ones. 7.5 per cent respondents have entered government services which points to the growing consciousness for white collar jobs among them. Even though departure from the caste-based occupation is itself no indication of change, yet it can be easily deduced from this that there is a movement from unskilled occupation to independent ones. This also means that the respondents do have the urge to get into better jobs and are willing to change their present jobs for better ones. Our study also shows that at least 29 out of 140 Chamars under study have given up tanning and taken to service. Tanning is undoubtedly an independent occupation and more lucrative than service. But the Chamar respondents have left it since it was an unclean pursuit which affected their social status; they have forsaken it for a less lucrative but socially more desirable occupation. The only caste which has remained unaffected by the currents of change is the Kanjar caste. It is equally important to note that the respondents in the third generation are losing their attraction for agricultural labour, and traditional occupations. But they do not show any desire for undertaking an industrial enterprise, they want to go in for trades and business. The respondents feel that the present change in their attitudes is on account of frequent contact with the urban people and sustained interest of the governmental agencies. Their proximity to such influences has been furthered by the rapid growth of means of transport and communication. However, aspiration for children's jobs is quite high and points to an urge of social climbing.

Economic Changes

In the field of economic change the 'Doms', 'Nat', 'Kanjars', 'Bansphors', and 'Musahars' are still lagging behind other castes and have not made any advance towards getting jobs outside their village. They remain still glued to their traditional occupations. The 'Chamars', 'Dhobis', 'Khatiks', 'Baheliyas', and 'Pasis' have, however, made considerable headway in this regard and with their hard labour are emerging as successful farmers and tradesman and, thus, playing the role of leaders. The Chamars, Dhobis, Baheliyas, Khatiks and Pasis seems to be more change-oriented and more free from the grip of traditionalism.

As against these castes, the 'Doms,' 'Kanjars', 'Musahar', 'Nats', and 'Bansphors', are yet not such change-oriented; they till take pride in doing their economic pursuits with their outdated tools and equipment. 160 respondents (40 per cent) have not made any significant change. This slow change is due their indifference and lack of proper thinking.

Data in hand also indicate that the Chamars, Khatiks, Baheliyas, Pasis and Dhobis (in all 60 per cent of the total respondents) have availed themselves better of the new opportunities for development. Among these the Chamars, Dhobis, Khatiks and Baheliyas have shown greater urge for social climbing and have considerably improved their social status. Dhobis according to the new list, have been included in the category of backward classes.

Considerable difficulty is being experienced by the welfare agencies in introducing the new programmes. Very few persons are enthusiastic about taking up trade and industry. Some scheduled caste members now read hidden political motives of the government in the welfare plans. Enthusiasm is languishing on account of the lack of sustained state interest.

A fairly large number of the scheduled castes have been benefitted by the transfer of land under the Zamindari abolition system. This has improved their economic condition and has also made them conscious of their own identity. In consequence, the subservient loyalty that they used to owe to the former land lords has declined. The landlords have also become aware of this fact and at places their mutual relations have become strained.

The progress made in obtaining land through imposition of ceiling on present holding does not seem to have made any salutary effect on the fate of the scheduled castes. Allotment of lands to landless scheduled castes has been insignificant. Land collected in Bhoodan has not been distributed to them so far. As far the civil or other higher government services are concerned, no scheduled caste members have been able to obtain them. However, the Chamar respondents have shown their eagerness for progress despite their enforced isolation and paucity of resources.

The scheduled castes feel anguished of dire poverty, yet they seem to be restless to get rid of it and other kinds of indigence which they had suffered for long. The problem in this respect again is one of the choice between rigid or obstinate adherence to social beliefs and acceptance of new values in store. On the one hand they are very firm and, indeed, very frank in sustaining their convictions about their occupation, trade and industry while on the other hand they want to improve their lot by undertaking smaller enterprises, but since they lack enterprise, they withdraw from the field.

The amount spent on the welfare of the scheduled castes and

the backward classes sector in the Five Year Plans is quite good and sufficient at the all India level.

The present investigator's visits to the scheduled castes living in different villages and suburban areas have given him an impression similar to that of Srinivas and Chopra that vast and rapid strides of change are taking place in our countryside. The scheduled castes after having become the owners of their land feel elevated and a sense of belongingness to the land has rapidly grown among them. They take now much interest in their land, its cultivation and crops. Above all, they get joy in doing hard labour because they now know that the crop is solely their own. Our conclusions, however, differ from those of Cohen, who found that abolition of Zamindari and adoption of various measures for the uplift of low caste people had not resulted in any significant improvement in the social status.

However, the size of indebtedness among the scheduled castes seems neither alarming nor enormous. In the fathers' generations, they were much affected by indebtedness but in the respondents' own generation, the situation seems to have changed considerably. Only 82.5 per cent are indebted in the present while 97.5 per cent were indebted in the fathers' generation. The Doms, Chamars, Dhobis, Musahars, Bansphors, Kanjars and the Nats are indebted mostly on account of their addiction to liquor. Customs of marriage, death and hospitality also force them to take credit. They, even to-day, depend largely upon the local grocer for loans. The reasons are that the grocer extends loan on easy terms. As regards the recovery of loans only 5.25 per cent respondents complained that the money lenders resorted to unscrupulous methods for recovery.

For a satisfactory solution of the unemployment problem, we cannot look to land alone. The area under study has good prospects for the development of certain small scale industries notable among them being consumer goods industries and processing industries. Palash leaves industry is one which can be developed successfully. Besides, poultry farming and fishery can also be introduced. Processing of maize, bee-keeping, rope making, net making and soap making have also scope for expansion. These industries can be a secondary source of employment to the scheduled castes who own land also. For those who have no land these can be the primary source of employment.

Change in the field of Education

There is an upward movement among the respondents in the field of educational attainments. In the grandfathers' generation, their attainments were not even worth-mentioning. However, in the fathers' generation, 2 fathers (0.50 per cent) had primary education while 398 respondents' fathers (99.50 per cent) had no education at all. This indicates that the tradition of not allowing the scheduled castes in the temples of education has disappeared. The informants revealed that there was no discrimination against their admission in the primary, junior, higher secondary schools and other colleges or universities. They further revealed that they had no occasion to register any complaint with the authorities about any prejudice. They also admitted that their children were getting scholarships although they were not sufficient in amount and not timely either.

The social education classes run by the Harijan Welfare Department or by Community Development Blocks (CDB) have not played the role that they were expected to play. The respondents reported that no government welfare agencies except malaria units had visited them and attended to their grievances. On account of a similar indifference on the part of other governmental agencies 79.50 per cent illiteracy still pervades among them. However, some of the respondents regretted their inability to take advantage of these programmes (literacy programmes) as they had no time for such classes, even if they were conducted. In the sowing harvesting periods they could not attend the night classes because they were overstrained due to manual labour in the fields. However, they appreciated the literacy programme launched for their benefit.

The respondents did not show any enthusiasm for women's education. They are afraid that female education will create hindrance in the performance of domestic duties.

Assistance to scheduled castes includes grant of stipends, scholarships, feeship, mid-day meals, uniforms, exemption from payment of examination fee, book grants and hostel facilities. In the third plan about 17.19 lakh stipend/scholarships were awarded to scheduled castes and likewise mid-day meals were supplied to 3.49 lakh scheduled caste students. The number of scholarships awarded has shown a phenomenal increase at the all India level over the years. In 1951-52 only 1,604 scheduled caste students got post-matric scholarships, but by 1955-56 their number had risen to 78,548. In 1966-67 the number of scholarship awarded increased further to 90,481.

The district Jaunpur has also registered an increase in the number of scheduled caste students getting scholarships. The following figures furnish the details of scholarships being awarded to the Harijan students in the different types of schools in the year 1970.

Degree class	150
Inter	820
B.T.C.	77
X class	344
IX class	344
VIII class	116
VII class	116
VI class	112
Total	5631

Political Changes

The Panchayat Raj and adult franchise have brought considerable awakening among the scheduled castes under study. They are becoming conscious of their democratic rights. However, there is no visible independent political awareness among them. The educated youths seem to have deflected towards the Arjak Sangh, but not in real earnest. The respondents usually reposed their confidence in the Congress Party because it had not only given them ample promises but was also fulfilling them.

In the 1967 general elections, in one constituency the scheduled castes stood behind a Jan Sangh candidate while in another constituency they threw in their lot with the Congress party. But in the mid-term poll the loyalties of the Harijans were clustered round the Jan Sangh Party. In the elections the respondents favoured those candidates who could manage to procure liquor and other drink for them or could give them help in the form of cash or promise 52.5 per cent respondents exercised their right of voting in the general elections held before 1967 while only 47.5 per cent went to the two polls i.e. 1967 general elections and the mid-term polls. 3 respondents (0.75 per cent) out of 400 are working as Pradhans of the Gram Sabhas, and one respondent (0.25 per cent) is an M. L. A. and another (0.25 per cent) is a Block Pramukh. In the panchayat sittings they are offered seats and also served with soft drinks. The respondents do not seem to be affiliated to any political party. However, two of their leaders—one from Dhobi caste and another from the Chamar caste are members of the legislative assembly while one Chamar is a member of the Lok Sabha (an M.P.).

The caste Hindus have now started looking at them as their legitimate competitors and thus, they try consciously to retain their hold through politicking. The upper castes who used to be the leaders of the polity and who obtained the support of the lower castes through sheer dominance and influence have revised their thinking. This development points to the evolution of the pluralistic tendencies in the village polity.

The formal institutions have, however, been able to do away with the popularity and sanctity of informal institutions notably the caste panchayats. They, even today, regulate the moral conduct of the members of a community. They set limits to dowry and to the number of persons to participate in a marriage party. They also arrange return of wives who have deserted their husbands.

Change in the Field of Health and Sanction

One of the prime necessities for the better up keep of man is the provision of safe drinking water. Most of the diseases can be attributed to contaminated water. The water facilities available to the scheduled castes are by no means adequate. The Musahars and Bansphors of Dhanipur (Jaunpur), Nats of Taraon village are experiencing considerable scarcity of drinking water. Their demand is, even today, unfulfilled.

The welfare agencies should meet their demand as early as possible. The government of Uttar Pradesh provides Rs. 1000 for the construction of a well as grants-in-aid. The arrangements for the rest of money is to be made by the parties concerned. For a hand pump, the amount granted is Rs. 225. It is only slackness on the part of the scheduled castes that they have not availed of this assistance.

At each step, the government cannot be blamed. Bringing health services within the reach of all and improving the standard of national health are not easy tasks by any manner of means. They require steadiness on the part of the government as patience on the part of the people. The national Tuburculosis Control Programme and the national Malaria Control Programme, Mass Veneral Disease Treatment campaign and the Leprosy Control Scheme have entered into their major operational phase through length and breadth of the country. The scheduled castes under study have greatly appreciated the anti-malaria campaign. The national water supply and sanitation programme has not undertaken the welfare work in the district of Jaunpur as yet. Side by side, we need a considerable number of maternity establishments and health centres in the district.

Housing

Sufficient funds are sanctioned for the construction of houses for scheduled castes both in urban and rural areas. In the district of Jaunpur colonies for certain castes have been constructed. The Kanjars, Doms (few) and Chamars of Kheradinganj (Marihau) and Khetasarai are now living in these colonies. But many Dom families are still living in slums. The municipality of Jaunpur should take immediate steps to clear the slums in the city. The Government of India, Ministry of Works, Housing and Supply provides adequate financial assistance to state governments and through them to municipal and local bodies for the clearance of Slum areas. The financial aspect of assistance is 37.5 per cent of the approved cost as outright subsidy in metropolitan cities, 37.5 per cent as loan by the centre and the remaining 25 per cent to be borne by the state government.

The village housing scheme of the Ministry of Works, Housing and Supply during the second five-year plan proposed to cover 5,000 villages all over the country. Besides, detailed technical advice and guidance is provided free of cost to the villagers by the Rural Housing Cells a field staff under the Block Development authorities. None of the scheduled caste members have availed of such advice. Funds in the form of subsidy are provided to the Doms for the procurement of long boots, long brooms and the moving latrines. It is very much astounding to note that no Dom family has tried to avail itself of the facility, Reasons : they are actually not aware of these facilities and secondly, they are shy of pressing of their problems for immediate disposal. Third, they rather avoid going to the authorities on account of their inferiority complex.

Legal Protection and Change

Legislative and executive measures in respect of land tenure, fundamental rights, social justice and education, have been enforced to safeguard the interest of scheduled castes in the various states. The Zamindari Abolition Act, the Untouchability Act 1955 and Acts of 1955-56 on marriage and inheritance have further strengthened the rights of the scheduled castes. Our findings in this regard are that under Untouchability Offences Act 1955 no person was arrested. Begari, has vanished, although 'Harwahi Partha' has raplaced it. No specific steps have been taken to protect the Scheduled castes from the exploitation of money lenders. On account of Zamindari abolition, they have now become the owners of land and as a result a sense of belongingness to land has developed among them. Thus, legal guarantees have proved to them as a boon.

Reservation Quota

Despite reservation quota in all India Central and State services, the scheduled castes under study have not been able to get into either of them. However, they aspire for better jobs for their children. Nirmal Kumar Bose, the Commissioner for scheduled castes and tribes in his annual report for 1969 presented the following recommendations for the speedy development of scheduled castes in various fields :

1. Appointment of lady social workers for effective propoganda,
2. Weaning away of the scheduled castes from traditional caste based occupations;
3. Increase of reservation quota upto 50 per cent i.e. 50 per cent vacancies should be reserved;
4. Setting up of Co-operative Societies for scavengers for their economic development.

However these recommendations have not been accepted so for by the Government. There is however every possibility of the proposal regarding reservation quota being opposed by the general public since it takes away a large slice of the services from the deserving and meritorious.

The second point may be raised here is ; have the special privileges granted to Harijans tended to foster security, self-pride and self independence among them ? There is no doubt that such facilities and special privileges have enabled them the better to solve their problems and have also been benefitting their children. But it may also be pointed out that these privileges have gone some way towards augmenting the sense of inferiority among the scheduled castes. Depending so much on government initiative, the Harijan will be isolated from the main stream of life and their personal initiative will be killed. R. Achutan is right when he maintains that the Harijan leaders have acquired a vested interest in keeping the untouchables backward and isolated from the main stream of Hindu life. Achutan sounded the warning that if Harijans themselves wanted to remain Harijans for evea, their uplift will for ever remain an illusion. The official agencies have no doubt an important role to play in securing the integration of the scheduled castes with the upper castes of the Hindu society without disturbing their essential harmony of life. But it should not be forgotten that unless the former are themselves prepared to share the new responsibilities according to their capacities no real advancement can take place in their position.

Conclusion

Indian society has always been dynamic in character; it did not preclude the mobility upward as well as downward of individual castes in the social hierarchy. For our support we have the historical facts that during the Maratha upheaval and after, the Brahmans entered the profession of arms. In the Mughal period, the Marathas and the Mahars both were, performing duties quite different from their original caste duties. Thus, the caste system was flexible enough to allow occupational change. Therefore it would not be correct to say that change is a result of modern forces alone. What the modern forces have done, in fact is that they have accelerated the process of mobility. If the scheduled castes lagged behind, the reason surely has been that they were deprived of educational, social and economic opportunities. Dube arrives at the same conclusion on the basis of his study of the 8 scheduled caste respondents among the 300 cases studied by him. He says that these castes are stripped off the basic conditions of social mobility.

It is a significant fact that the scheduled castes have been passing through a phase of evolutionary transformation. New situations have been pressing them to accept their challenge. The tendency towards professionalism in the coming generation has taken root and aspirations for high positions have been aroused. The new situations have left the scheduled castes in a transition followed by stresses and strains.

The new changes their growing social proximity, and the legal guarantees now available to them have paved entirely a new way for the scheduled castes. The distinction between the cultural and structural dimensions of caste has been minimised. Untouchability stands abolished under law and its practice in any form is forbidden.

The new opportunities created by the British rule resulted in greater social mobility from which the scheduled castes also benefitted a great deal. During the post independence period, the increased attention paid to the scheduled castes and backward classes, further strengthened the trend towards social mobility among them. An important feature of this trend is the manner in which the members of these castes have been working for the improvement of the economic and social conditions of their castes men. The successive generations of scheduled castes under study have steadily striven to change their hereditary occupations for economically more rewarding and socially more prestigious ones. The trend started in the grandfathers' generation, was maintained in the fathers' generation and became more pronounced in the third generation. Notable among the factors which are responsible for the socio-economic transformation of these castes are the welfare programmes, new transportation facilities and their growing political awareness. The land settlement schemes, new social legislations, and the various constitutional provisions for their welfare have gone a long way towards removing their backwardness.

It is rather a fortunate coincidence that the evaluation of the various welfare schemes relating to the problems of the scheduled castes has been carried out in detail by the Estimates Committee of Parliament. The study team on social welfare and welfare of the backward classes set up by the committee on Plan Projects of the Planning Commission and the sub-committees set up by the Central Harijan Board, such as the scavengers committee and the Untouchability Committee, 1965 headed by Illa Pyrema, I have gone into various other aspects of their problems. The proper execution of their recommendation (submitted in 1969) regarding the establishment of 'Finance Corporations' for financing the scheduled caste members is, indeed very sound. It has been emphasized by the committee that Finance Corporation should be able to play a big role improving the economic conditions of the Harijans. R. Achutan, a member of the same committee has rightly reacted to the manner in which the disbursement of grant-in-aid through intermediary agencies is made. He says that a few persons at the top have made it customary to draw money from the central funds in the name of charitable institutions which they squander at their own discretion. This sort of benefit to the higher echelons in the name of Harijans should be stopped because it encourages nepotism and corruption.

Regular reports by the welfare agencies have been submitted in the past, but follow-up work has been seldom undertaken to remove the short falls. Here are a few suggestions for improving the condition of the scheduled castes.

Carrying out of night soil as headloads by the Dom should be immediately stopped. The municipalities should take the necessary steps for the implementation of the same. Better it would be that the recommendations of the Malkani Commission. with regard to flush latrines in the urban areas are introduced forthwith. The Japanese type of wheel barrows can be utilised for the removal of night soil. The Central Advisory Board for Harijans Welfare set up a sub-committee to investigate into this problem. The report of the Scavengers' Living Conditions Enquiry Committee published by the state of Bombay is a very useful guide for all municipalities to adopt its recommendations to improve the conditions at least of its conservancy staff.

The Doms of Jaunpur do not have any community centre nor do the Kanjars and the Nats, Bansfords and Musahars. The municipality of Jaunpur should bear the entire cost of erecting and establishing such centres for the Doms. For others the District Board may take the initiative. Such centres can be utilised for sewing and tailoring purposes as well as for recreational gatherings.

The scheduled caste boys can learn here new trades if these centres are properly organised and managed. The Harijan welfare department of Jaunpur should comply with the demand as early as possible. The Doms of Jaunpur have also claimed a share in the income accruing from the sale of refuse by the municipality. We suggest that a share should be paid to them for augmenting their income. The Nats of Taraon village have neither a well nor a hand pump for drinking water. Their demand for a pipe or well should also be attended to by the Harijan Welfare Department or by the community development programme. Both the departments should provide the necessary funds for digging a kucha well for the time being. Prejudices against the scheduled castes may still lurk in the minds of Hindu castes and they may eventually debar them from drawing water from the upper-caste wells. It is, therefore, necessary to avoid strictness in the execution of orders in order to prevent social conflicts.

Subsidies for fruit gardens to Khatiks and for poultry farming to Pasis need special attention. Jaunpur district is an ideal place for growing papaya, custard apple, musk melon and mango fruits. The area also shows promise for the cultivation of various types of vegetables; such as potatoe, carrot, spinach, brinjal, onion, radish and coriander. Jaunpuri radish is famous throughout the Uttar Pradesh for its size and taste. Poultry farming has, also a bright future for its culture. If properly started, it can yield larger income to the Pasis. The district provides a wide market for the sale of eggs. With the development of industries, there will be an ever increasing demand for milk, meat and eggs.

A concerted effort should be made by all non-official agencies (political, social and religious) to have a country-wide propaganda (aided by the government for the removal of untouchability). Recognised voluntary agencies are already being paid liberal grants by government for carrying on extensive propaganda for the general awakening and welfare of scheduled castes. For promoting social contact the following steps suggested in the report of the Commissioner for Scheduled Castes and Tribes are worth mentioning here and strict adherence to them would surely remove this social stigma from our society for ever.

1. Caste Hindus should be persuaded to give up untouchability by making practical efforts towards this end and not by empty precepts.
2. Opportunities and occasions should be explored for free mixing of Harijans and Caste Hindus.
3. Caste Hindu ladies should freely mix up with Harijan women to educate them and impart training to them in domestic occupations.
4. Caste Hindu students in their vacations should visit Harijan basties and educate their inhabitants. If possible, books and other reading material should be supplied free to Harijans.
5. In all the boarding houses and hostels, arrangements should be made for accommodating Harijan students.
6. The work of drawing water from common wells, etc. entry to shops, hostels and temples by the Harijans should be vigorously taken up. If necessary protection of law should also be sought.
7. Land should be granted for tilling purposes to landless Harijans.
8. Provision of house sites should be made for Harijans in both the rural and urban areas.
9. Introduction of mechanical and up-to date methods of clearing the latrines, sewers, drains etc. should be introduced and the inhuman practice of cleaning these by hands be given up.
10. Cottage industries of Harijans should be given protection and propaganda for the increased use of articles manufactured by them should be made.

The State of Uttar Pradesh should also draw up a special scheme for the removal of untouchability on the lines of the Bombay scheme which consists of the following :

1. Preparation of story films.
2. Prizes to villages which have shown outstanding work for its removal.

3. Grants to voluntary agencies to hold fairs should be floated.
4. Entertainment programmes by ballet singers.
5. Kirtans and dramas.
6. Encouragement of cosmopolitan hostels.

People's Participation in Welfare Programmes

There is, however, no denying the fact that legislation and recommendations alone cannot take us very far unless we are able to carry public opinion with us. The canker of untouchability will take time to disappear. It is, therefore, suggested that people should be mobilised through the technique of propaganda.

Allotment of Land

While allotting land to the scheduled castes either from the Bhoodan side or from other agencies priority should be accorded to the following :

1. The allotted land or land already owned by the scheduled castes should not be allowed to be transferred to non-scheduled castes under any circumstances.
2. Normal water charges for ten years and onwards may be charged.
3. While allotting waste land to them they should be allowed a period of at least three years for its development before they are asked to pay land revenue to the Government. No levy should be imposed on them during the first year and in the second and third year only 1/3 and 2/3 respectively be charged.
4. The land allotted should not be less than 5 acres of dry land or 2.5 acres of wet land.
5. The taccavi loans should be paid to these persons as far as possible.
6. Surplus land that will be available in rural areas as a result of legislation prescribing ceiling on holdings should be allotted to scheduled castes on a preferential basis. While alloting surplus or cultivable waste land, the

co-operative societies may have precedence but the land should not tied up with any such condition.

Industries

As regards the development of industries we need an effective organisation solely devoted to the task of survey, study, piloting and organisation of those industries which have prospects for an appreciable change in the situation. There is scope for expansion of bamboo work. For its proper development we require the establishment of production-cum-training centre in Dhanipur.

Co-operatives

In order to cater to the needs of the scheduled castes, the distribution of credit and necessaries should be entrusted to the co-operative marketing societies. The community development programmes can take up these steps alone with the Harijan Welfare Department at the district level. By expanding the programme of multi-purpose co-operative societies, the exploitation of the scheduled castes by unscrupulous dealers will be stopped. Societies like the Andhra Pradesh Scheduled Tribes Co-operative Finance and Development Co-operation Ltd. should be started in the different districts of the State of Uttar Pradesh. Andhra Pradesh has opened marketing depots at important market centres which collect produce from the farmers or traders and also sell the goods and services. While promoting or sponsoring co-operative organisation in the village we should be careful enough to see that the rich or influential sections of the people do not dominate the co-operatives and monopolise them for their benefit. The society should embrace all the avenues of economic development, such as agriculture, industry (village) and consumer goods. We, also, feel that special attention should be accorded to the preservation of fruits and vegetables grown and sold by the Khatiks in the district.

Education

The Governments are spending huge amounts on the education of the scheduled castes, but unless the Harijan boys, attend the school, the tangible results are not likely to be achieved. Their education should be made vocation-oriented. For a rapid change, steps for bringing girl's education on a par with men's should receive priority. The question of exempting scheduled castes gent circumstances from payment of tuition fee at all stages of education has already been taken up by the Ministry of Education with all the State Governments.

Representation in Local Bodies

The scheduled castes in the State of Uttar Pradesh have been guaranteed representation in all local bodies through statutory provision in the appropriate acts. In addition, provision has been made for a general reservation of 10 per cent of the vacancies for members of the scheduled castes in the town area committees. The question of housing facilities, security of land tenure and debt redemption and check on money lender are under the consideration of the state government. Thus all kinds of encouragement and assistance are being given to scheduled castes. But it is a matter of great regret that the scheduled castes in the district of Jaunpur have made little use of these facilities.

The services for which recruitment is made on all India basis, require higher educational qualification. Until therefore education has progressed sufficiently among the scheduled castes, it will not be possible for them to take full advantage of the reservation in their favour made in these services. Relaxation in regard to age limits for gazetted services vary from state to state. These should be made uniform. The reserved vacancies should be adequately publicised so that full advantage can be taken of them by the scheduled castes. Not all the scheduled castes read newspapers, those who live in the village have no access to mass media of communication. Therefore some method of publicity which can enable the villagers also to take advantage of the vacancies should be involved. Periodical checks may be made to find out if proper care is being taken to ensure the recruitment of scheduled castes against posts reserved for them. This will ensure that the scheduled castes get adequate representation in the services within the shortest possible time.

A Happy Future

The world of tomorrow will have a countenance fundamentally different from that of the one we live in to-day. The breath-taking increase of knowledge in natural science and technology, has revolutionized our conception of the world and life. It is therefore, indispensable in this forward rushing world that the word 'Harijan' which has become so derogatory and has created an unnecessary feeling of separateness between the caste Hindus and scheduled castes should be deleted and the upper and lower castes alike be treated as being parts of a single Hindu cultural entity. All should get equal opportunity to exercise their free choice and will and all should be allowed to enter into open competition with others. This move, if practised by all of us, will surely be an assest for our centuries of neglected and isolated brethern.

To conclude it will be very useful to expatiate on the need and further possibilites of research work. We need special studies in relation to education, health, housing and the economic development of the scheduled castes. Second, we can explore the impact of development programmes; such as, community development programmes and the Harijan welfare programmes and other national programmes, i.e. National Malaria Programme and Panchayat Raj, Harit Kranti on the scheduled castes.

A survey can be conducted to assess disparities existing between the scheduled castes and caste Hindus. The surveys will have to be done from the point of view of practical utility. We suggest that the government should conduct specific surveys in relation to specific problems. We have the problems like the Problems of rights in land etc. Research into these problems is an essential pre-requisite for effective planning.

Appendices

APPENDIX I

Scheduled caste Population, 1967

Sl. No.	*State*	*Population*
1.	Andhra Pradesh	4,973,616
2.	Assam	732,756
3.	Bihar	6,536,875
4.	Gujarat	1,367,255
5.	Jammu and Kashmir	268,530
6.	Kerala	1,422,057
7.	Madras (Tamil Nadu)	6,073,536
8.	Maharashtra	2,226,914
9.	Mysore	3,117,232
10.	Madhya Pradesh	4,253,000
11.	Orissa	3,763,858
12.	Punjab	4,139,106
13.	Rajasthan	2,359,640
14.	Uttar Pradesh	15,417,245
15.	West Bengal	6,950,726

Population of sche 'uled castes adapted from India, 1967, Publication Division, Ministry of Information and Broadcasting, Government of India. Section X and XXVI, pp. 1116 and 392, 490.

APPENDIX II

Percentage of Literacy by States & Social Categories, 1961

States	*General Population*	*Scheduled Castes*
India	24.0%	10.27%
Andhra Pradesh	21.2%	8.47%
Assam	27.4%	24.41%
Bihar	18.4%	5.96%
Gujarat	30.5%	22.46%
Jammu & Kashmir	11.0%	4.72%
Kerala	46.8%	24.44%
Madhya Pradesh	17.1%	7.89%
Tamil Nadu	31.4%	14.66%
Maharashtra	29.8%	15.78%
Mysore	25.4%	9.06%
Orrisa	21.7%	11.57%
Punjab	24.2%	9.64%
Rajasthan	15.2%	6.44%
Uttar Pradesh	17.6%	7.14%
West Bengal	29.3%	13.58%
Nagaland	17.9%	25.40%

Census of India, 1961, Vol. I, Part II-C (i), pp. 49-95 and Vol. I, Part V-A (i), p. 1.

APPENDIX III

Literacy Position Among Scheduled Castes by Sex and Rural/Urban Areas in 1961 and 1971—India, All age groups

(Figures in lakhs)

Year	Areas	Population			Literates			Illiterates		
		Persons	Male	Female	Persons	Male	Female	Persons	Male	Female
	All	644.17	329.17	315.00	66.16	55.81	10.35	578.01	273.36	304.65
	Areas				(10.27)	(16.95)	(03.29)	(89.73)	(83.05)	(96.71)
1961	Urban	68.70	36.47	32.33	14.98	11.74	3.24	53.72	24.73	28.99
	Areas				(21.80)	(32.19)	(00.05)	(78.20)	(67.81)	(89.95)
	Rural	575.47	297.70	282.77	51.18	44.00	07.11	524.29	248.63	275.66
	Areas				(8.89)	(15.06)	(02.51)	(91.11)	(84.94)	(97.49)
	All	800.5	413.43	386.62	117.34	92.44	24.90	682.71	320.99	361.72
1971	Areas				(14.67)	(22.36)	(6.44)	(85.33)	(77.64)	(93.56)
	Urban	95.56	50.77	44.79	27.37	19.76	7.61	68.19	31.01	37.18
	Areas				(28.64)	(38.92)	(16.99)	(71.36)	(61.08)	(83.01)
	Rural	704.49	362.66	341.83	89.97	72.68	17.29	614.52	289.98	324.54
	Areas				(12.77)	(20.04)	(5.06)	(87.23)	(79.96)	(94.94)

Figures in parentheses indicate % of the total population.

Source : Yojna, Vol. XXII/18, 1 October, 1978.

APPENDIX IV

Population Figures of Scheduled Castes Census, 1971

Sl. No.	*Name of State*	*Total population of scheduled castes (in lakhs)*	*Percentage of scheduled castes population*
1.	Andhra Pradesh	58.16	13.27
2.	Assam	09.13	6.10
3.	Bihar	83.86	14.28
4.	Gujarat	18.90	6.84
5.	Haryana	18.96	18.88
6.	Himachal Pradesh	8.08	22.23
7.	Jammu & Kashmir	3.81	8.30
8.	Karnataka	42.77	13.14
9.	Kerala	20.02	8.30
10.	Madhya Pradesh	57.52	13.09
11.	Maharashtra	31.77	6.00
12.	Manipur	0.16	1.53
13.	Meghalaya	0.04	0.38
14.	Nagaland	No SC	No SC
15.	Orissa	33.07	15.09
16.	Punjab	33.48	24.71
17.	Rajasthan	42.16	15.82
18.	Sikkim	0.10	4.76
19.	Tamil Nadu	73.38	17.75
20.	Tripura	1.93	12.34
21.	Uttar Pradesh	190.95	21.00
22.	West Bengal	89.00	19.90
23.	Andaman & Nicobar	No SC	No SC
24.	Arunachal Pradesh	0.03	0.10
25.	Chandigarh	0.29	11.30
26.	Dadar & Nagarhaveli	0.01	1.80
27.	Delhi	6.36	15.60
28.	Goa, Daman & Diu	0.17	1.90
29.	Laksha Dweep	No SC	No SC
30.	Mizoram	No SC	No SC
31.	Pondicherry	0.73	15.50
		Total 8.25 crores	

The latest population of the scheduled castes based on the Scheduled Castes Amendment Orders Act, 1976.

APPENDIX V

*Percentage of landless Agricultural Labourers and Cultivators Among Scheduled castes**

Census year	*Percentage of landless Agricultural labour*	*Per cent of land holding cultivators*
1961	34.5	37.8
1971	51.8	27.9

Decennial percentage increase (+) 9.9
or decrease (—) +17.3

* *Source* : The 20th Report on the C SC/ST, 1975-76 and 1976-77.

APPENDIX VI

Atrocities Reported in the office of the C SC/ST

Year	*Murder*	*Rape*	*Burning*	*Beating*	*Untouchability*
1974	114	127	320	637	601
1975-76	49	13	13	604	44
1976-77	18	4	4	566	36

Others	Total
1974-959	2758
1975-76	723
1976-77	626

APPENDIX VII

*Disposal of cases reported to police and registered under the Untouchability (Offences) Act, 1955 the Protection of Civil Rights Act, 1976**

Year	Registered with police	Convicted	Acquitted	Compounded	Pending
1971	526	91	96	138	114
1972	1515	631	253	233	299
1973	2949	1207	312	388	449
1974	1908	669	247	288	384
1975	3528	936	480	611	561
1976	3099**	86	360	155	1997

* *Source*: Reports of the Commissioner for the Scheduled Castes and Scheduled Tribes for 1975-76, and 1976-77.

** Figures relate to only three states of U.P , Maharashtra and Gujarat only.

Notes : (i) The Protection of Civil Rights Act, 1976 has strengthened the rights of the Harijans for social utilities.

(ii) The Dalit Literary Movement (DLM) in Maharashtra has been reaffirming the solidarity of Harijans and rejuvenating their ideological commitments and helping in formulating their further policies and strategies.

APPENDIX VIII

*Progressive representation of Scheduled Castes in All India Administrative Service, India**

Year	Total No.	Scheduled castes	Percentage
1956	1197	17	1.42
1957	1253	18	1.43
1958	1521	29	1.90
1959	1651	35	2.12
1960	1700	38	2.24
1961	1737	39	2.24
1962	1794	46	2.56
1963	1908	68	3.56
1964	2002	81	4.04
1965	2105	96	4.56
1966	2211	114	5.15
1967	2339	128	5.43
1968	2459	153	6.22
1969	2626	166	6.32
1970	2687	178	5.70
1971	2754	188	6.82
1972	—	—	—
1973	—	—	—
1974	—	—	—
1975	—	—	—
1976	3237	277	8.56

All India Administrative Services Position on 1st Jan., 1979 appeared in India, 1980.

		Scheduled castes	Scheduled Tribes
1979	IAS	355	160
—	IPS	207	78

Bibliography

Ghurye, G. S. : Caste and Race, 1932 Popular Book Depot, Bombay, The Scheduled Castes and Scheduled Tribes.

Ambedkar, B. R. : Who were the Shudras (1946).

Singh, Mohindra : The Depressed Classes 1947 Hind Kitabs Ltd.; Bombay.

The Govt. of India Act, 1935 Section 279.

Raja Ram Mohan Roy : English Works 1828.

Farquhar, J. N. : Modern Religious Movements in India (1915).

Dr. Purohit, B. R. : Hindu Revivalism and Indian Nationalism, 1965.

Dayananda Saraswati : Satyarth Prakash.

Dayananda Commemoration Volume : A tribute.

Chhajju Singh : The life and Teachings of Swami Dayananda, Addison Press (1903).

Nargolkar, V. S. : Removal of Untouchability : Goals and Attainments. The Indian Journal of Social Work, October, 1968 Vol. No. XXX Number 3.

Singh, S. : New Dimensions of Untouchability : A Brief Survey, Social Welfare (Hindi) February, 1970.

The Hindu, December 24, 1932.

Forbes, James : Oriental Memories, 1934.

Barve, V. N. : How far it is true (Article) Social Welfare (Bombay) June 12, 1941 quoted in Mohindra Singh's book: The Depressed classes.

Hutton, J. H. : Caste in India, Cambridge (1946).

The Untouchability Act, 1955 (Act No. XXII of 1956).

Census of India, 1921, Vol. I, Part I, Para 193.

Franchise Committee of 1919.

Nair Central Committee, 1929.

Hartog Committee's Report.

Census Report of India, 1961.

Harold R. Issacs : India's Ex-Untouchables, (1965).

Sen Devi, P. L. : Welfare of the Scheduled Castes & Scheduled Tribes in Kerala, Social Welfare, January, 1971.

A Preliminary Appraisal of the Scheduled Castes of India, Office of the Registrar, General India, New Delhi.

Government of India, Ministry of Law (Legislative Department).

Government of India, Ministry Home Affairs.

Notification No. SRO 2477 A the 29th October, 1956.

Trevelyan, G. M. : English Social History, 1944.

Patrudu, B. V. S. : Scheduled Castes in India : Social Progress and Social Legislation. Social Welfare January, 1971.

Haig Woolseley : Cambridge History of India, Vol. III (The Sultanate Period).

Nehru, Jawahar Lal : Discovery of India.

Sachau, Edward C. : Alberuni's India (1910).

Baines, A. : Ethnography (Castes & Tribes), 1932.

Briggs, G. W. : The Chamars, 1920.

Kane, P. V. : History of Dharmshastras.

Census Report 1891.

District Gazetteer of Jaunpur.

Kirkpatrick, W. : Primitive Exogamy and the Caste System in Proceedings, A & B Vol. No. 3, Calcutta, 1912.

Turner : Caste in the Kumaon Division and Tehri Garhwal State (in the Report of Census of India, 1931) Vol. I Part III BPP 17 Sqq.

Crook : Tribes castes II S. V. Dom.

Rose : Tribes and castes.

U. P. Census, 1911,

Nesfield, J. C. : Brief View of the Caste System of the North Western Provinces and Oudh (1885).

Srimat Bhagavat : Part II, Gita Press, Gorakhpur.

Hamilton, F. : Buchnan, Edinburgh.

Martin, M. : The History of Antiquities Topography and Statistics of Eastern India, 1838.

O'Malley, L.S.S. : Indian Castes, Customs (1932).

Lowie, Robert, H. : Marriage in Encyclopaedia of Social Sciences, Vol. X.

Ibbetson, Denzil (1880) : The Races, Castes and Tribes of the People, 1883 (Reprints of the Census of the Punjab 1881).

Bernard, Cohen S. : The Chamars of Semapur (1954) Unpublished Ph. D. dissertation.

Henry H. Johnson : Sociology : A Systematic Introduction (India Edition). 1966, Bombay Allied Publishers.

Bogegamage A. and P. V. Veeraghavan : Status Images in Changing India, Bombay Manaktala (1967).

Bhatia, H. S. : Intercaste relations and Aspirational Levels—An Attitude Study : Indian Journal of Social Work, Vol. XXX No. 1 April 1970.

Aiyappan, A. : Social Revolution in a Kerala Village. A Study in Cultural Change (1965).

Srivastava, A. L. : Attitude Towards Harijans Yet to Change Social Welfare, October, 1970.

Taya Zinkin : In a Tanjore Village.

Dube, S. C. : Indian Villages, Routledge and Kegan Paul (1955).

Srinivas, M. N. : Caste in India Modern, Social Change in Modern India, 1962.

Ninth Report of the Commissioner for Scheduled Castes and Scheduled Tribes Sec. V. (1959-60).

Merton, Robert, K. : Social Theory and Social Structure.

Sorokin, P. A. : Social and Cultural Mobility, (1959).

Miller, S. M. : Comparative Social Mobility.

Ghurye, G. S. : Caste and Occupation (1961). Popular Book Depot, Bombay.

Roy Burman, B. K. : Social Mobility Movements Among Scheduled Castes and Tribes Govt. of India Press, New Delhi 11.

The All India Rural Credit Survey Report, (1954).

Report of the Committee of Co-operative Credit (S. N. 18).

Report of the Working Group on Co-operative Farming Vol. I (Ministry of Community Development and Co-operation).

The U. P. Zamindari Abolition and the Land Reform Act, 1950.

Report on Agricultural Labour in India, Vol. I (Published by the Ministry of Labour and Employment, Govt. of India).

Srikant, L. M. : Report of the Commissioner for Scheduled Castes and Scheduled Tribes for 1953.

India 1960 compiled by the Ministry of Information Broadcasting, Govt. of India.

A study by the Programme Evaluation Organisation.

Harijan Social Welfare Office, Jaunpur, A Report.

Singh, R. D. : Social Change in a U. P. village for Eastern Quarterly December, 1956.

Singh, Y. : Changing Power Structure of Village Community. A case study of Six Villages in Eastern U. P. in Rural Sociology In India by A. R. Desai, Bombay 1961.

Majumdar, R. C. : Panchayats in India.

Mukerjee, Radhakumud : Local Government in Ancient India (1919) Oxford Clarendon Press.

Dhillon, H. (1955) : Leadership and groups in a South Indian Village, New Delhi, Planning Commission Programme Evaluation Organisation, Govt. of India.

Oscar Lewis : Village life in Northern India.

Prabhat Chandra : Rural Leadership in India, The Eastern Anthropologist, September, 1959.

Vidyarthi, L. P. : Leadership in India.

Singh, H. : Strains in Leadership Structure (From Status Group to Pluralism in an east U. P. Village in Economic and Political Weekly, May 3, 1969.

Wildavaski : Leadership in a Small Town, (1964).

Opler, M. E. : Factors of Traditions and Change in a Local Election in Rural India.

Park, R. & Tinker, I. : Change in Leadership and Political Institutions in India.

Times of India, November 18, 1970.

David G. Mandelbaum : Social Organisation and Planned Culture Change in India.

Selig H. Harrison : India : The Most Dangerous Decades Ch. VI (1960).

Roy, Ramashray : Congress Defeat in Farrukhabad (1955).

The Hindustan Times (daily), March 29, 1970.

Five Year Plans.

Yojna April 5, 1970 (A weekly—Planning Commission).

Harijan Welfare in U. P. published by Harijan Welfare Directorate, U. P. Lucknow.

Report of the Commissioner for Scheduled Castes and Scheduled Tribes (1959-60).

Annual Report on Scheduled Castes and Tribes, May 15, 1969.

Untouchability Committee, 1965 (Its report published in 1969).

Ghurye, G. S. : Caste in India.

Dube, S. M. : Social Mobility Among the Professions in A City in Transition (1967).

Marc Galanter : Changing Legal Conception of Caste (A paper prepared on Religion and politics in South India held in Colombo in July, 1964).

Malkani Commission on Public Health and Hygiene.

Srikant, L. M. : Fourth Annual Report of the Commissioner for Scheduled Castes and Tribes (1954).

Srikant, L. M. : Recommendation of 9th Report of the Commissioner for Scheduled Castes and Tribes (1959-60).

Lynch, O.M. : The Politics of Untouchability—A Case from Agra, India, Columbia University Press, New York.

Srinivas, M. N. : Changing Institution and Values in Modern India, Economic Weekly; Annual Review, Feb. 1962.

K. Ranga Das : Rural Leadership and Conflict Study of an Andhra Village, Economic and Weekly, Vol. III, No. 17, April 17, 1967, p. 67.

T.K. Oommen : Strategy for Social Change—A Study of Untouchability, Economic and Political Weekly, Vol. III, No. 5, June 22, 1968, p. 935.

N. J. Usha Rao : Deprived Castes in India (A Profile of Karnataka) Chugh Publications (1981) Allahabad.

Uttam Bharti and Anuradha Bharti : The Dalit Sahitya Movement in Maharashtra : A Sociological Analysis, Sociological Bulletin, Vol. 26, No. I. March, 1977.

Singh, Soran : Abstract of Thesis : Indian Dissertation Abstracts (CSSR), January-March, 1976, New Delhi.

Singh, Soran : Occupations mobility Among Scheduled Castes—The Indian Journal of Social Work, October, 1976, Vol. XXXVII, No. 3, p. 267, Bombay.

Singh, Soran : The Scheduled Castes : New Dimensions of Social Change—Indian Journal of Comparative Sociology, Vol. III, No. 1, February, 1977, p. 28 Dharwar, Karnataka.

Singh, Soran : A Study of Inter Caste Relations and Social Distance Among Scheduled Castes—Indian Journal of Social Research, Vol. XIX, Nos. 1, 2 & 3, April, August, December, 1978 pp. 160-163 Meerut.

Singh, Soran : Indebtedness of Scheduled Castes—The Eastern Anthropologist: No. 32, Vol. 2, April-June, 1979.

Singh, Soran : Marriage Customs Among Scheduled Castes—Mosaic of Warming Session, Roorkee XV Indian Sociological Conference, Meerut, Nov. 1980.

Singh, Soran : Social Distance Among Scheduled Castes in Rural U. P. (Panel I weaker Sections of Society) Agriculture Sector in Mosaic of Sociological Inquiries Vol. I, Indian Sociological Conference, 1980, Meerut.

Singh, S. : Reform Movements Among Scheduled Castes (All India Sociological Conference, Meerut, 1980.

Jagjiwan Ram : Caste Challenge in India, Vision Books, New Delhi, 1980.

Ranga Rao, K. : Village Politics, Popular Prakashan Bombay, 1980.

Khan, Mumtaz Ali : Scheduled Castes & Their Status in India, Uppal Publications House, New Delhi, 1980.

C. Pervathamma : The Weaker Sections of Society—The Scheduled Castes in India, Sociological Bulletin March, 1981 Vol. 30, No. 1.

Index